lonely planet

SAN ANTONIO, AUSTIN & TEXAS BACKCOUNTRY

ROAD TRIPS

This edition written and researched by

Amy C Balfour, Lisa Dunford
Mariella Krause, Regis St Louis
and Ryan Ver Berkmoes

HOW TO USE THIS BOOK

Reviews

In the Destinations section:

All reviews are ordered in our authors' preference, starting with their most preferred option. Additionally:

Sights are arranged in the geographic order that we suggest you visit them and, within this order, by author preference.

Eating and Sleeping reviews are ordered by price range (budget, midrange, top end) and, within these ranges, by author preference.

Map Legend

Routes

- Trip Route
- Trip Detour
- Linked Trip
- Walk Route
- Tollway
- Freeway
- Primary
- Secondary
- Tertiary
- Lane
- Unsealed Road
- Plaza/Mall
- Steps
- Tunnel
- Pedestrian Overpass
- Walk Track/Path

Boundaries

- International
- State/Province
- Cliff

Population

- Capital (National)
- Capital (State/Province)
- City/Large Town
- Town/Village

Transport

- Airport
- Cable Car/Funicular
- Parking
- Train/Railway
- Tram
- Underground Train Station

Trips

- 1 Trip Numbers
- 9 Trip Stop
- Walking tour
- Trip Detour

Highway Route Markers

- 97 US National Hwy
- 5 US Interstate Hwy
- 44 State Hwy

Hydrography

- River/Creek
- Intermittent River
- Swamp/Mangrove
- Canal
- Water
- Dry/Salt/Intermittent Lake
- Glacier

Areas

- Beach
- Cemetery (Christian)
- Cemetery (Other)
- Park
- Forest
- Reservation
- Urban Area
- Sportsground

Symbols In This Book

✓	Top Tips	🍷	Food & Drink
🔗	Link Your Trips	🌳	Outdoors
	Tips from Locals	📷	Essential Photo
↪	Trip Detour	🏃	Walking Tour
📖	History & Culture	🍴	Eating
👨‍👧‍👦	Family	🛏	Sleeping

- 👁 **Sights**
- 🏖 **Beaches**
- 🏃 **Activities**
- 🤿 **Courses**
- ☞ **Tours**
- 🎆 **Festivals & Events**
- 🛏 **Sleeping**
- 🍴 **Eating**
- 🍷 **Drinking**
- ☆ **Entertainment**
- 🔒 **Shopping**
- 🛈 **Information & Transport**

These symbols and abbreviations give vital information for each listing:

- ☏ Telephone number
- ⊘ Opening hours
- P Parking
- ⊝ Nonsmoking
- ❄ Air-conditioning
- @ Internet access
- 🛜 Wi-fi access
- 🏊 Swimming pool
- 🥗 Vegetarian selection
- 📖 English-language menu
- 👶 Family-friendly
- 🐾 Pet-friendly
- 🚌 Bus
- ⛴ Ferry
- 🚊 Tram
- 🚆 Train
- apt apartments
- d double rooms
- dm dorm beds
- q quad rooms
- r rooms
- s single rooms
- ste suites
- tr triple rooms
- tw twin rooms

CONTENTS

Hill Country Horse riders at sunset

WELCOME TO
SAN ANTONIO, AUSTIN & TEXAS BACKCOUNTRY

AS BIG AS TEXAS IS, the only way to truly appreciate it is to hit the road and find out what's out there in those wide, open spaces. The cities have tons to offer, but Texas also does 'small town' like few other states, with friendly locals, historic buildings, quirky claims to fame, and an easygoing way of life everywhere you look.

So what's your pleasure? Fields of wildflowers and rolling hills in the land of Lady Bird Johnson? Beaches and seafood along the Gulf or smoky brisket in the Barbecue Capital of Texas? An epic journey from the Mexico border to the Texas panhandle? Or intriguing desert landscapes with surprising stops along the way, culminating in an enormous national park?

Whatever route you choose, saddle up for adventure on a grand scale.

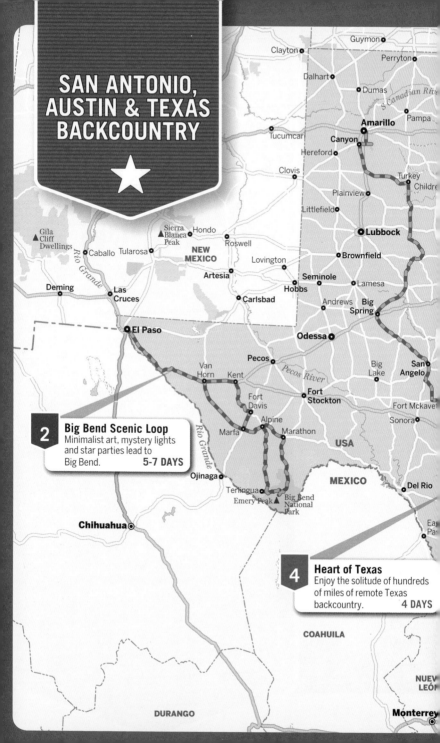

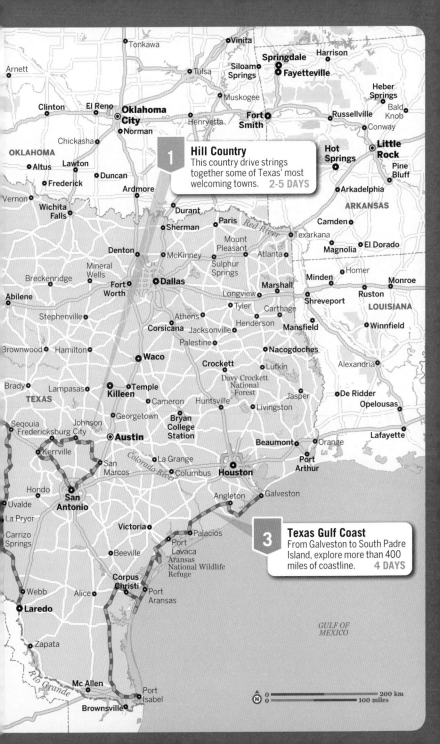

1 **Hill Country**
This country drive strings together some of Texas' most welcoming towns. **2-5 DAYS**

3 **Texas Gulf Coast**
From Galveston to South Padre Island, explore more than 400 miles of coastline. **4 DAYS**

GULF OF MEXICO

0 — 200 km
0 — 100 miles

DAVE HUGHES / GETTY IMAGES ©

Big Bend National Park
(left) Everyone knows Texas is huge. But you can't really appreciate just how big it is until you visit this national park. See it on Trip 2

San Antonio Riverwalk
(above) Cafe after bar after restaurant after bar: the Riverwalk is a mighty entertaining experience. Outdoor stages host frequent events and there are hotels aplenty to rest your head. See it on Trip 1

Gruene (right) Scoot across a well-worn wooden floor at Texas' oldest dance hall. See it on Trip 1

CITY GUIDE

SAN ANTONIO

Tourism has been good to San Antonio and the sprawling city reciprocates with a wide variety of attractions to keep everyone entertained. In addition to its colorful European-style Riverwalk lined with cafes and bars, it rewards visitors with a well-rounded menu of museums, theme parks, outdoor activities and historical sites.

Getting Around

San Antonio can be daunting for drivers, and parking is no treat either. Yet the city is laid out in a grid system (albeit a little skewed at times), making navigation a little easier on the nerves. Pay close attention to highway signs, especially when they indicate a left-hand exit – miss one of those and you're in for a nickel tour of the surrounding suburbs.

Parking

Street parking is hard to find but there are plenty of public parking lots, including at most of the major hotels. You can park for free at the **VIA Ellis Alley Park & Ride** (between E Crockett and Center Sts), then pay $4 roundtrip to ride downtown. Ask for a parking transfer on the bus and put it in the slot to 'pay' when you exit the garage. Parking at **Market Square** is relatively inexpensive, while **Riverbend Garage** (a little more expensive) puts you in the heart of things.

Above San Antonio Riverwalk

Where to Eat

The Riverwalk offers easy pickings for a touristy dinner and drinks. South St Marys and S Alamo Sts in the Southtown and King William districts also host a good number of eateries. Look for hole-in-the-wall Mexican joints scattered the length of N Flores St.

Where to Stay

San Antonio has a plethora of hotel rooms, so you have plenty of choices in the downtown area. The city also has its fair share of B&Bs, which are generally good value, ensconced in fine old homes in the more historical areas of the city.

Useful Websites

Convention & Visitors Bureau (www.visit sanantonio.com) For loads of useful planning info.

San Antonio Current (www.sacurrent.com) For entertainment and event listings.

Express-News (www.mysanantonio.com) For local news.

Trips through San Antonio:

Destination Coverage: p58

AUSTIN

With its quirky, laid-back vibe and its standing as Live Music Capital of the World, Austin is one of the decade's definitive 'it' cities. Watch live music every night, stroll funky South Congress, dig into spicy Tex-Mex and tangy barbecue, and meet some of the friendliest people you'll find.

Getting Around

Downtown is easy to get around, and since Austin is pretty spread out, most everybody drives. However, you can always catch a Capital Metro bus (single ride $1) or take a taxi ($2.40 per mile) if you can find one – or call **Yellow Cab** (☎512-452-9999).

Parking

Aside from downtown and campus, parking is usually plentiful and free. Downtown meters (25c for 15 to 20 minutes) run late on weekends, including Sunday.

The parking garage at 1201 San Jacinto is free for two hours and $2 per hour after that, maxing out at $8.

Above Texas State Capitol (p73), viewed from South Congress

Where to Eat

Top restaurants are scattered all over town, but South Congress has the best concentration of interesting eateries. For cheap meals on the go, try the food trailer enclaves on South Congress, East 6th and Waller Sts, or S First and Elizabeth Sts. For Tex-Mex and a fun vibe, try the ever-popular **Güero's Taco Bar** (☎512-447-7688; 1412 S Congress Ave; mains $6-15; ⏱11am-10pm).

Where to Stay

Downtown has everything from high-end chains to the historic Driskill Hotel to the Firehouse Hostel. Chains in every price range are found along I-35. South Congress (SoCo) has some quirky and cool digs. Look for bed and breakfasts in the Hyde Park area.

Useful Websites

Austin CVB (www.austintexas.org) Detailed travel planning.

Austin 360 (www.austin360.com) Listings, listings and more listings.

Austin Chronicle (www.austinchronicle.com) Events calendar from the local weekly.

Destination Coverage: p72

NEED ^{TO} KNOW

CELL PHONES

The only foreign phones that work in the the USA are GSM multiband models. Cell-phone reception can be spotty in rural areas.

MONEY

ATMs widely available. Credit cards are accepted in most hotels and restaurants.

TIPPING

Standard is 15% to 20% for waiters and bartenders, 10% to 15% for taxi drivers and $1 to $2 per bag for porters.

TIME

All but two far-west Texas counties are in the Central Time Zone (GMT/UTC minus five hours)

FUEL

Gas stations are ubiquitous in urban areas and along interstates. They can be few and far between in isolated areas.

RENTAL CARS

Avis (www.avis.com)

Enterprise (www.enterprise.com)

Hertz (www.hertz.com)

IMPORTANT NUMBERS

AAA (☏ 800-222-4357)

Emergency (☏ 911)

Road Conditions (☏ 511)

Climate

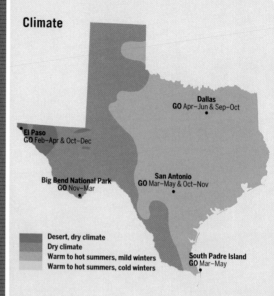

Dallas
GO Apr–Jun & Sep–Oct

El Paso
GO Feb–Apr & Oct–Dec

Big Bend National Park
GO Nov–Mar

San Antonio
GO Mar–May & Oct–Nov

South Padre Island
GO Mar–May

Desert, dry climate
Dry climate
Warm to hot summers, mild winters
Warm to hot summers, cold winters

When to Go

High Season (Jun–Aug)

» Kids are out of school, so attractions are busiest.

» Temperatures will be stiflingly hot outside, but everywhere inside has air-con.

» Prime time for beaches, lakes and rivers.

Shoulder Season (Mar–May & Sep–Nov)

» Best time of year to travel: the weather is less intense, everything is still open.

» This is when most festival planners throw events, including rodeos.

» A second shoulder season lasts from September through early November.

Low Season (Dec–Feb)

» Some theme parks and such closed for the season.

» North Texas occasionally freezes, south Texas rarely does.

» Christmastime festivities statewide.

Your Daily Budget

Budget: Less than $100

» Campgrounds and hostels: $12–58

» Taquerias, sidewalk vendors, supermarkets for self-catering: $5–12

» Share a rental car; split cost of park vehicle entry fees: $13–20

Midrange: $100–250

» Mom-and-pop motels, low-priced chains: $60–100

» Diners, good local restaurants: $8–20

» Visit museums, theme parks and national and state parks: $5–25

Top End: Over $250

» Boutique hotels, B&Bs, resorts, national-park lodges: $120–300

» Upscale restaurants: $18–63

» Hire an outdoor outfitter; take a guided tour; book ahead for top performances: from $25

Eating

Roadside diners Simple, cheap places with limited menus.

Taquerias and food stands Outdoor stalls selling tacos, frybread and Sonoran hot dogs.

Farm-to-Table In mountain towns and big cities, the focus is increasingly on fresh and local.

Vegetarians Options can be limited in cattle country, but most cafes have vegetarian options.

Eating price indicators represent price of a main dish:

$	less than $10
$$	$10–20
$$$	more than $20

GET INSPIRED

William Least Heat-Moon's road trip classic, *Blue Highways: A Journey into America* (1982), relates the tale of his long, circular journey around America in a Ford van named 'Ghost Dancing'. Following only 'blue highways' – off-the-beaten-track back roads, so called because they used to be colored blue on old highway maps – he encounters a cast of eccentric characters as he explores the culture of small-town USA.

Sleeping

B&Bs Quaint accommodations, usually include breakfast.

Motels Affordable options, typically outside downtown.

Camping Facilities for tents, often at state and national parks. Some also offer simple cabins.

Resorts Popular in warm, sunny cities and beautiful backcountry areas; often have spas.

Price indicators represent the cost of a double room:

$	less than $100
$$	$100-200
$$$	more than $200

Arriving in Texas

Dallas–Fort Worth International Airport

Train You can take the Dallas Area Rapid Transit (DART) orange line directly downtown for $2.50.

Taxis Cost about $40 to $60

Shuttles SuperShuttle runs services to downtown and major hotels with fares from $18.

Dallas Love Field

Train Take DART's Love Link 524 that connects to Inwood/Love Field Station, where you can pick up the orange line or green line.

Taxis Cost about $40 to $60

Shuttles SuperShuttle runs

services with fares from $18.

Houston Airport System

See p106.

Austin-Bergstrom International Airport

See p80.

San Antonio International Airport

See p64.

Useful Websites

TravelTex (www.traveltex.com) State's official tourism website, where you can request the free *Texas Travel Guide*.

Lonely Planet (www.lonely planet.com) Summaries, travel news, links and traveler forum.

Texas Highways (www. texashighways.com) Travel magazine with extensive festival and event listings.

Texas Parks & Wildlife (www.tpwd.state.tx.us) A complete guide to Texas' outdoor recreation and environment.

For more, see Driving in Southwest USA (p124).

TEXAS BARBECUE

Beef brisket

Make no bones about it – Texas barbecue is an obsession. It's the subject of countless newspaper and magazine articles, from national press including the *New York Times* to regional favorite *Texas Monthly*. Some of central Texas' smaller towns maintain reputations for their smokehouse cultures, and routinely draw dedicated pilgrims from miles around.

No self-respecting Texan would agree with another about who has the best barbecue, since that would take the fun out of it. But most do see eye to eye on a few things: brisket is where a pit master proves his or her reputation; seasoning is rarely much more than salt, pepper and something spicy; and if there's a sauce, it's probably made from ketchup, vinegar and the drippings of the wood-smoked meat.

The best Texas barbecue often comes from famous family dynasties that have been dishing up the same crowd-pleasing recipes for generations. Telltale signs that you've located an authentic barbecue joint include zero decor, smoke-blackened ceilings, and laid-back table manners (silverware optional). At most places, you can order a combination plate or ask for specific meats to be sliced by the pound right in front of you. Of course, there are variations on this nowadays, but in Texas, where barbecue baiting is a bit of a pastime, some swear this down-home style is the only way.

However you like it – sliced thick onto butcher paper, slapped on picnic plates, doused with a tangy sauce or eaten naturally flavorful right out of the smokehouse barbecue pit – be sure to savor it...and then argue to the death that your way is the best way. Like a true Texan.

History

The origins of central Texas barbecue can be traced to 19th-century Czech and German settlers, many of whom were butchers. These settlers pioneered methods of smoking meat, both to better preserve it (before the advent of refrigeration) and also to tenderize cuts that might otherwise be wasted.

Credit also goes to Mexican *vaqueros* (Spanish-speaking cowboys), especially in Texas' southern and western borderland regions, who dug the first barbecue pits in about the 16th century, then grilled spicy meats over mesquite wood. African Americans who migrated to Texas brought with them recipes for a 'wet' style of barbecue, which involved thick marinades, sweet sauces and juicier meats.

Somewhere along the way, slow-smoked barbecue crossed the line from simple eating pleasure to statewide obsession. Maybe it's the primal joy of gnawing tender, tasty meat directly from the bone, or the simplistic, sloppy appeal of the hands-on eating experience. Whatever the reason, dedicated barbecue eaters demonstrate nearly religious devotion by worshipping at the pits of Texas' renowned smokehouses.

Cook-Offs

There are people who will travel the entire state of Texas to sample all the various permutations of barbecue. But if your time's a little more limited, you can always try one of the many organized cook-offs around the state. Amateurs and pros alike come together for the noble joint cause of barbecue perfection and, if they're lucky, bragging rights. Cook-offs generally start on Friday afternoon so the pit masters have plenty of time to get their meat just right before the judging on Saturday, even if it means staying up all night. (You can't rush these things.) Once the judging is complete, the public is invited to swoop in and judge for themselves.

One of the largest events is the **Taylor International Barbeque Cook-off** (www.taylorjaycees.org), held in late August in Taylor (northeast of Austin), with up to 100 contestants competing in divisions including beef, ribs, pork, poultry, lamb, seafood and wild game. If you can't make that one, a quick search on www.tourtexas.com will lead you to events such as the Good Times Barbecue Cook-off in Amarillo or the Wildfire Barbecue Cook-off, Car Show & Festival in Bowie.

Otherwise, check out the calendar on the **Central Texas Barbecue Association** (CTBA; www.ctbabbq.com) website, where you can also read the incredibly detailed rules that competitions must follow ('CTBA recommends the use of a Styrofoam tray with a hinged lid and without dividers or the best readily available judging container that is approximately 9 inches square on the bottom half').

Ingredients

In today's Texas, barbecue recipes are as varied as central Texas summers are long. Most folks agree on the basics: slow cooking over a low-heat fire. A cooking time of up to 12 or 16 hours isn't unheard of – anything less and you're just too darn impatient. It allows the meat to be infused with a rich smoky flavor of usually hickory or pecan in the eastern part of the state, oak in central Texas and mesquite out west. (Mesquite was considered all but a weed until someone realized how nice a flavor it lent to wood chips.)

- - - - - - - - - - - - - - - - - - - -

The Meat

Texas barbecue leans heavily toward beef – a logical outgrowth of the state's cattle industry – and most signature dishes come straight from the sacred cow. The most common is beef brisket, a cut often used for corned beef. With a combination of patience, experience and skill, a seasoned pit boss can transform this notoriously tough meat into a perfectly smoked, tender slab of heaven. Even tougher cuts of meat enter the smokehouse and emerge hours later, deeply flavorful and tender to the tooth. Sliced thin and internally moistened by natural fat, a well-smoked brisket falls apart with the slightest touch and can rival more expensive cuts for butter-smooth consistency.

Carnivores seeking a more toothy challenge can indulge in beef ribs – huge meaty racks that would do Fred Flintstone proud – or relax with a saucy chopped-beef sandwich. Word to the wise: if you need to stay presentable, think twice about the ribs, which tend to be a full-contact eating experience (even as part of a three-meat sampler plate).

Lone Star State cattle worship stops short of excluding other meats from the pit. The noble pig makes appearances in the form of succulent ribs, thick buttery chops and perfect slices of loin so tender they melt on the tongue. In recent years chicken has shown up on the menu boards, mainly to provide beginners with a non-hoofed barnyard option. Traditionalists, however, stick with the good stuff – red meat and plenty of it.

Every self-respecting barbecue joint will also serve sausage. Texas hot links, the peppery sausage of regional renown, is created with ground pork and beef combined with pungent spices. Although it's not technically in the barbecue family, sausage is cooked over the same fire so has the same smoky flavor. If nothing else it makes an excellent meat side dish to go alongside your meaty main dish.

The Rub

Everyone knows that the word 'barbecue' is usually followed by the word 'sauce.' But not so fast, there. Good barbecue is more than just meat and sauce. The other key component is the rub, which is how the meat is seasoned before it's cooked. There are wet rubs and dry rubs. A dry rub is a mixture of salt, pepper, herbs and spices sprinkled over or painstakingly rubbed into the meat before cooking. A wet rub is created by adding liquid, which usually means oil, but also possibly vinegar, lemon juice or even mustard.

WHERE TO EAT TEXAS BBQ

San Antonio
County Line Smokehouse (☎210-229-1941; www.countyline.com/CountyLineRiverWalk. html; 111 W Crockett St, Riverwalk, San Antonio; sandwiches $11-13, platters $15-29; ☺11am-10pm Sun-Thu, to 11pm Fri & Sat) This outpost of the Austin minichain scratches the itch nicely with heaping dishes of brisket, ribs and sausages.

Austin
Lamberts (☎512-494-1500; 401 W 2nd St, Austin; mains $14-42; ☺11am-2pm & 5:30-10pm) Torn between barbecue and fine dining? Run by Austin chef Lou Lambert, Lambert's serves intelligent updates of American comfort-food classics.

Salt Lick Bar-B-Que (p78)

Hill Country
Black's Barbecue (p27)

Kreuz Market (p27)

Lum's (☎325-446-3541; 2031 Main St, Junction; mains from $8; ☺8am-11pm Mon-Sat) One of the region's best barbecue joints.

Fannin
McMillan's BBQ (☎361-645-2326; 9913 US 59, Fannin; mains from $6; ☺10am-3pm Mon-Wed, 10am-8pm Thu-Sun) Close to the Fannin battleground site, this small roadhouse is loved for its sweet and savory barbecue.

Houston
Gatlin's (www.gatlinsbbq.com; 1221 W 19th St, Houston; sandwiches $8, mains $12-15; ☺11am-3pm & 5-9pm Mon-Sat) Houston's best barbecue. The Houston Press says so, and we wouldn't argue otherwise. But watch your timing; not only are their hours limited, they sometimes sell out.

Midland
KD's Bar-B-Q (☎432-683-5013; http://kdsbarbq.com; 3109 Garden City Hwy/TX 158, Midland; mains from $12; ☺11am-9pm Tue-Sat) If you had to go to one Texas 'cue joint, this would do. This rambling place is east of town, just off I-20 at exit 138.

El Paso
Rib Hut (☎915-532-7427; www.ribhutep.com; 2612 N Mesa St, El Paso; mains $8-20; ☺11am-10pm Mon-Sat, noon-9pm Sun) Join the UTEP (University of Texas at El Paso) crowd over a serious plate of ribs.

Applied like a paste, a wet rub seals in the meat's natural juices before cooking. This key step is just as important as the slow cooking in getting the flavor just right.

The Sauce

Wisdom about barbecue sauce varies widely from region to region and sometimes joint to joint. There's huge debate over what kind, how much or whether you need it at all. In Lockhart, Kreuz Market's meat is served without any sauce at all, and it's so naturally juicy and tender you'll agree it's not necessary. But excellent sauce-heavy barbecue is divine as well. We'll leave it up to you to make up your own mind.

Texas barbecue sauce has a different flavor from other types – that's why it's Texas barbecue, y'all. It's not as sweet as the kind you'll find gracing the tables of barbecue joints in Kansas City and Memphis – more a blend of spicy and slightly sweet. There are thousands of variations and no two sauces are exactly alike, but recipes are usually tomato based with vinegar, brown sugar, chili powder, onion, garlic and other seasonings.

The Sides

Side dishes naturally take second place to the platters of smoked meat. Restaurant-style sides usually include pinto beans, potato salad or coleslaw, while markets sometimes opt for simpler accompaniments like onion slices, dill pickles, cheese slices or whole tomatoes. (If your meat is served on butcher paper, the sides will come in a bowl or on a plate.)

Etiquette

The first question that comes to most people's mind is, 'How do I eat this without making a mess?' You don't. Accepting the fact early on that barbecue is a messy, messy venture will give you the attitude you need to enjoy your meal. One coping mechanism is to make a drop cloth of your napkin. Bibs haven't exactly caught

Salt Lick Bar-B-Que (p78)

on in the barbecue world – this is a manly meal, after all – but tucking your napkin into your shirt is never frowned upon, especially if you didn't come dressed for it.

Which leads to another question: How does one dress for barbecue? First off, don't wear white. Or yellow, or pink, or anything that won't camouflage or coordinate with red. At 99% of barbecue restaurants (the exception being uppity, nouveau 'cue) you will see the most casual of casual attire, including jeans (harder to stain) and shorts, and maybe even some trucker hats.

Whether you eat with your hands or a fork depends on the cut of the meat. Brisket and sausage are fork dishes, while ribs are eaten caveperson-style. (It also depends on the restaurant. Kreuz Market doesn't offer forks. As the owner famously says, 'God put two of them at the end of your arms.') If you're eating with your hands, grab extra napkins. You might also be provided with a small packet containing a moist towelette, which will at least get you clean enough to head to the restrooms to wash up.

A final thought on etiquette: if you're at a restaurant that uses a dry rub and you don't see any sauce, it's probably best not to ask – it would be a bit like asking for ketchup to put on your steak.

Road Trips

On the road to Chisos Basin, Big Bend National Park (p37)
DENIS JR. TANGNEY / GETTY IMAGES ©

Hill Country

1

Take a drive through the countryside where gently rolling hills are blanketed with wildflowers, friendly folks enjoy an easy way of life, and there's plenty to do along the way.

TRIP HIGHLIGHTS

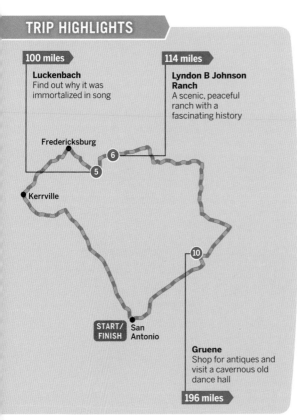

100 miles

Luckenbach
Find out why it was immortalized in song

114 miles

Lyndon B Johnson Ranch
A scenic, peaceful ranch with a fascinating history

Fredericksburg

Kerrville

START/FINISH — San Antonio

Gruene
Shop for antiques and visit a cavernous old dance hall

196 miles

2–5 DAYS
229 MILES / 368KM

GREAT FOR...

BEST TIME TO GO
In March and April for wildflower season.

 ESSENTIAL PHOTO

Bluebonnets – pose your kids or yourself in a field full of wildflowers.

 BEST FOR CULTURE

Two-stepping at Texas' oldest dance hall in Gruene.

1 Hill Country

In March and early April when wildflowers are blooming, this is one of the prettiest drives in all of Texas — perfect for a day trip or a lazy, meandering vacation. Along this route, you can rummage through antique stores, listen to live music, dig in to a plate of barbecue, and learn about the president who called this area home.

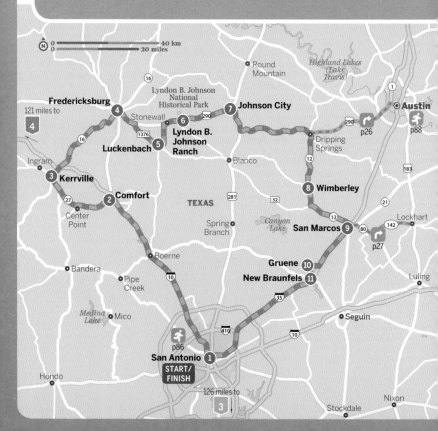

① San Antonio (p58)

While sprawling San Antonio isn't part of the Hill Country, it's a great launching point for your trip. Don't miss the lovely, European-style Riverwalk, a paved canal that winds its way through downtown and is lined with colorful cafes, hotel gardens and stone footbridges. For the best overview, hop on a Rio San Antonio **river cruise** (p59), a 40-minute ride that loops through downtown, or take our walking tour, p86.

Pay your respects at the **Alamo** (p58), where revolutionaries fought for Texas' independence from Mexico.

The Drive » Head northwest on I-10 to get to Comfort, less than an hour from downtown San Antonio. When the

wildflowers are blooming, detour north on Waring-Welfare Rd then back on TX 27.

② Comfort (p66)

Remarkably under the tourist radar, Comfort is a 19th-century German settlement and perhaps the most idyllic of the Hill Country bunch, with rough-hewn limestone homes from the late 1800s and a beautifully restored historic center in the area around High and 8th Sts.

Shopping for antiques is the number-one activity, but you'll also find a few good restaurants, a winery and, as the town's name suggests, an easy way of life. Start at the **Comfort Antique Mall** (☏830-995-4678; 734 High St; ⊙10am-5pm Sun-Fri, to 6pm Sat) where you can pick up a map of antique stores, or go to the **Comfort Chamber of Commerce** (www.comfort-texas.com) website for options.

The Drive » The interstate is a straight shot, but we prefer the back road of TX-27 west to Kerrville that takes you through serene farmland.

③ Kerrville (p67)

The Hill Country can feel a bit fussy at times, but not Kerrville. What it lacks in historic charm, it makes up for in size, offering plenty of services for travelers,

as well as easy access to kayaking, canoeing and swimming on the Guadalupe River. The best place to hop in the water is beautiful **Kerrville-Schreiner Park** (2385 Bandera Hwy; day-use adult/child/senior $4/1/2; ⊙8am-10pm). The park's concession stand rents inner tubes (per day $4) and four-person canoes (per hour from $7) for lazy floats along the river.

While you're in town, check out one of the world's best collections of cowboy art at the **Museum of Western Art** (p67). The building itself is beautiful, with handmade mesquite parquet floors and unique vaulted domes overhead, and it's chock-full of paintings and sculptures depicting scenes from the Old West.

The Drive » Take TX 16 northeast of town for half an hour to get to Fredericksburg.

④ Fredericksburg (p70)

The unofficial capital of the Hill Country, Fredericksburg is a 19th-century German settlement that specializes in 'quaint.' The town packs a lot of charm into a relatively small amount of space, with a boggling array of welcoming inns and B&Bs, and a main street

LINK YOUR TRIP

3 Texas Gulf Coast

From San Antonio, drive 143 miles south along Hwy 37 to reach the coastal town of Corpus Christi.

4 Heart of Texas

From Kerrville, travel 149 miles northwest to San Angelo.

lined with historic buildings housing German restaurants, *biergartens*, antique stores and shops.

Many of the shops are typical tourist-town offerings, but there are enough interesting stores to make it fun to wander. Plus, the town is a great base for checking out the surrounding peach orchards and vineyards. Just a few miles east of town, **Wildseed Farms** (www.wildseedfarms.com; 100 Legacy Dr; h9:30am-5pm) has cultivated fields of wildflowers and sells seed packets along with just about every wildflower-related gift you can imagine.

The Drive ›› Five miles southeast of town on US 290, turn right on Ranch Rd 1376 and follow it 4.5 miles into Luckenbach. There are only a handful of buildings, so don't worry that the actual town is somewhere else.

TRIP HIGHLIGHT

⑤ Luckenbach (p71)

You won't find a more laid-back place than Luckenbach, where the main activity is sitting at a picnic table under an old oak tree with a cold bottle of Shiner Bock and listening to guitar pickers, who are often accompanied by roosters. Come prepared to relax, get to know some folks, and bask in the small-town atmosphere.

Start at the old trading post established back in 1849 – now the **Luckenbach General Store** (p71), which also serves as the local post office, saloon and community center. Out back you'll find the picking circle, and there's often live music on the weekends in the old dance hall; go online to check out the town's **music schedule** (www. luckenbachtexas.com).

DETOUR: AUSTIN

Start: ⑦ Johnson City

Since this trip is all about winding your way through the Hill Country, we didn't list Austin as a stop. After all, it warrants its own whole trip, which we hope your central Texas itinerary already includes.

However, we'd be remiss if we didn't mention that, when you get to Dripping Springs, you're only half an hour from the Texas state capital. If you go, check out the walking tour on p82.

The Drive ›› Take Luckenbach Rd back north to US 290. The LBJ Ranch is just 7 miles down and the entrance is right off the highway.

TRIP HIGHLIGHT

⑥ Lyndon B Johnson Ranch

You don't have to be a history buff to appreciate the family home of the 36th president of the United States. Now the **Lyndon Johnson National Historic Park** (www.nps.gov/lyjo; Hwy 290; park admission & driving tour free, house tour $3; ◷9am-5:30pm, house tours 10am-4:30pm), this beautiful piece of Texas land is where Lyndon Johnson was born, lived and died.

The park includes the Johnson birthplace, the one-room schoolhouse where he briefly attended school and a neighboring farm that now serves as a living history museum. The centerpiece of the park is the ranch house where LBJ and Lady Bird lived, and where he spent so much time during his presidency that it became known as the 'Texas White House.'

You can also see the airfield that he and other foreign dignitaries flew into, the private jet he used as president and the Johnson family cemetery, where LBJ and Lady Bird are both

DETOUR:
LOCKHART

Start: ❾ San Marcos

People travel from all over the state to dig into brisket, sausage and ribs in Lockhart, officially designated in 1999 as the Barbecue Capital of Texas. Lucky for you, you only have to detour 18 miles to experience the smoky goodness. You can eat very well for less than $13 at the following places:

Black's Barbecue (215 N Main St; sandwiches $6-11, brisket per pound $16; ⏲10am-8pm) A longtime Lockhart favorite since 1932, with sausage so good Lyndon Johnson had Black's cater a party at the nation's capital.

Kreuz Market (☎512-398-2361; 619 N Colorado St; brisket per pound $17, sides extra; ⏲10:30am-8pm) Serving Lockhart since 1900, the barnlike Kreuz Market uses a dry rub. This means you shouldn't insult them by asking for barbecue sauce; – Kreuz doesn't serve it, and the meat doesn't need it.

Chisholm Trail Bar-B-Q (☎512-398-6027; 1323 S Colorado St; lunch plates $8, brisket per pound $12; ⏲8am-8:30pm) Like Black's and Kreuz Market, Chisholm Trail has been named one of the top 10 barbecue restaurants in the state by *Texas Monthly* magazine.

Smitty's Market (208 S Commerce St; lunch plates $7, brisket per pound $12; ⏲7am-6pm Mon-Sat, 9am-6.30pm Sun) The blackened pit room and homely dining room are all original (knives used to be chained to the tables). Ask to have the fat trimmed off the brisket if you're particular about that.

buried under sprawling oak trees.

Stop by the visitor center to get your free park permit, a map and a free CD audio tour.

The Drive » LBJ's childhood home is just 15 minutes east on US 290.

---

❼ Johnson City (p72)

You might assume Johnson City was named after President Johnson, but the bragging rights go to James Polk Johnson, a town settler back in the late 1800s. The fact that James Johnson's grandson went on to become president of the United States was just pure luck.

Here you'll find **Lyndon Johnson's Boyhood Home** (100 E Ladybird Lane; ⏲tours half hourly 9am-11:30 & 1-4:30pm), which Johnson himself had restored for personal posterity. Park rangers from the **Visitor Center** (cnr Ladybird Ln & Ave G; ⏲8:45am-5pm) – where you can also find local information and exhibits on the president and first lady – offer free guided tours every half hour, which meet on the front porch. On the surface, it's just an old Texas house, but it's fascinating when you think about the boy who grew up here.

The Drive » Follow US 290 south toward Blanco then east toward Dripping Springs. At Dripping Springs, turn right on Ranch Rd 12 towards Wimberley.

---

❽ Wimberley (p81)

A popular weekend spot for Austinites, this artists' community gets absolutely jam-packed during summer weekends – especially on the first Saturday of each month from April to December, when local art galleries, shops and craftspeople set up booths for **Wimberley Market**

WHY THIS IS A CLASSIC TRIP
MARIELLA KRAUSE, AUTHOR

Easily accessed from both San Antonio and Austin (my hometown), the Hill Country is a popular getaway for both its natural beauty and easygoing nature. You can drive this entire loop in under five hours, but what's the rush? There are so many great little towns and interesting things to do, you'll be glad you decided to linger.

Above: Luckenbach General Store (p26)
Left: Rope swing, Blue Hole
Right: Oak tree in Hill Country

Days (www.shopmarketdays. com; 601 FM 2325; parking $5; ⊙7am-4pm 1st Sat of month), a bustling collection of live music, food and more than 400 vendors at Lion's Field on RR 2325.

For excellent scenic views of the surrounding limestone hills near Wimberley, take a drive on FM 32, also known as the **Devil's Backbone**. From Wimberley, head south on RR 12 to FM 32, then turn right toward Canyon Lake. The road gets steeper, then winds out onto a craggy ridge – the 'backbone' – with a 360-degree vista.

Afterwards, cool off at Wimberley's famous **Blue Hole** (☎512-847-9127; www.friendsofbluehole.org; 100 Blue Hole Lane, off CR 173; adult/child/under 4yr $8/4/ free; ⊙10am-6pm Mon-Fri, to 8pm Sat, 11am-6pm Sun), one of the Hill Country's best swimming holes. It's a privately owned spot in the calm, shady and crystal-clear waters of Cypress Creek. To get here from Wimberley, head down Hwy 12 south of the square, turn left on County Rd 173, and then after another half-mile, turn onto the access road between a church and cemetery.

The Drive » Keep going south on Ranch Rd 12; San Marcos is about 15 minutes southeast through some more (mostly) undeveloped countryside.

SAN ANTONIO, AUSTIN & TEXAS BACKCOUNTRY **1** HILL COUNTRY

SCENIC DRIVE: WILDFLOWER TRAILS

You know spring has arrived in Texas when you see cars pulling up roadside and families climbing out to take the requisite picture of their kids surrounded by bluebonnets – Texas' state flower. From March to April in Hill Country, Indian paintbrushes, wine cups and bluebonnets are at their peak.

Check the **Wildflower Hotline** (☎800-452-9292) to find out what's blooming where. Taking Rte 16 and FM 1323, north from Fredericksburg and east to Willow City, is usually a good route.

⑨ San Marcos (p81)

Around central Texas, 'San Marcos' is practically synonymous with 'outlet malls,' and bargain shoppers can make a full day of it at two side-by-side shopping meccas. It's not exactly in keeping with the spirit of the Hill Country, but it's a popular enough activity that we had to point it out.

The fashion-oriented **San Marcos Premium Outlets** (p83) is enormous – and enormously popular – with 140 name-brand outlets. Across the street, **Tanger Outlets** (p83) has more modest offerings with brands that aren't that expensive to start with, but it's still fun to hunt.

The Drive ≫ Shoot 12 miles down I-35 to the turnoff for Canyon Lake. Gruene is just a couple miles off the highway.

TRIP HIGHLIGHT

⑩ Gruene (p83)

Get a true taste of Texas at **Gruene Hall** (www.gruenehall.com; 1280 Gruene Rd; ⊗11am-midnight Mon-Fri, 10am-1am Sat, 10am-9pm Sun), a dance hall where folks have been congregating since 1878, making it Texas' oldest. It opens early, so you can stop by anytime to toss back a longneck, two-step on the well-worn wooden dance floor, or play horseshoes out in the yard. There's only a cover on weekend nights and when big acts are playing, so at least stroll through and soak up the vibe.

The town is loaded with antique stores and shops selling housewares, gifts and souvenirs. **Old Gruene Market Days** are held the third weekend of the month, February through November.

The Drive ≫ You don't even have to get back on the interstate; New Braunfels is just 3 miles south.

⑪ New Braunfels (p84)

The historic town of New Braunfels was the first German settlement in Texas. In summer, visitors flock here to float down the Guadalupe River in an inner tube – a Texas summer tradition. There are lots of outfitters in town, like **Rockin' R River Rides** (☎830-629-9999; www.rockinr.com; 1405 Gruene Rd; tubes $20). Its rental prices include shuttle service, and for an additional fee it can also hook you up with an ice chest and a tube to float your ice chest on.

The Drive ≫ From New Braunfels it's 32 miles on the I-35 back to San Antonio.

Right: Tubing on the Guadalupe River, New Braunfels

Big Bend Scenic Loop

2

Although it's known for wide open spaces, west Texas is packed with surprising experiences that make this a supremely well-rounded drive.

TRIP HIGHLIGHTS

231 miles
Marfa
Home of art installations and the Marfa Lights

210 miles
Fort Davis
Nighttime star parties at the observatory are stellar

START/ FINISH
El Paso

Alpine

385 miles
Terlingua
This thriving ghost town is one of a kind

357 miles
Big Bend National Park
Mile after mile of scenic hiking trails

5–7 DAYS
535 MILES / 860KM

GREAT FOR...

BEST TIME TO GO
Best between February and April – before the heat sets in.

ESSENTIAL PHOTO
Prada Marfa, a quirky roadside art installation.

BEST FOR OUTDOORS
McDonald Observatory's night-time star parties.

eft: A celestial show in clear, dark skies at McDonald Observatory (p35)

2 Big Bend Scenic Loop

Getting to visit Big Bend National Park and experiencing the endless vistas straight out of an old Western are reason enough to make this trip. But you'll also get to have plenty of fun along the way, exploring the quirky small towns that are prime road trip material. West Texas offers an unforgettable set of experiences, including minimalist art installations, nighttime astronomy parties and thriving ghost towns.

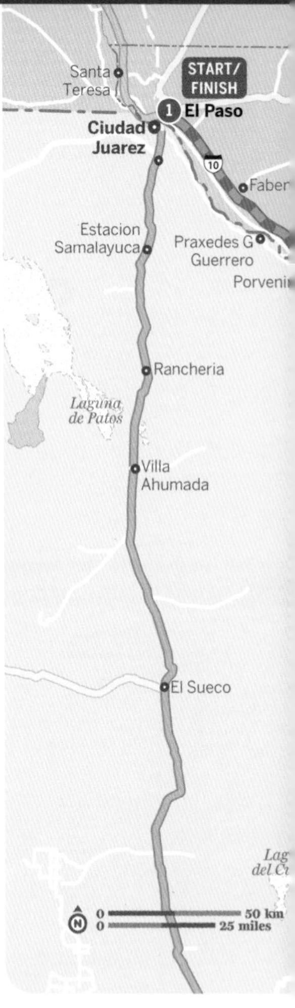

---

❶ El Paso (p90)

Start your trip in El Paso, a border city that's wedged tightly into a remote corner of west Texas. Before you get out of town, take advantage of the great Mexican food you can find all over the city – it's right across the river from Mexico – and take time to enjoy some of El Paso's many free museums. Downtown, the **El Paso Museum of Art** (☎915-532-1707; www.elpasoartmuseum.org; 1 Arts Festival Plaza; special exhibits charge admission; ☺9am-5pm Tue-Sat, to 9pm Thu, noon-5pm Sun) has a terrific Southwestern collection, and the engaging modern pieces round out the display nicely.

Another one you shouldn't miss is the **El Paso Holocaust Museum** (www.elpasoholocaustmuseum.org; 715 N Oregon St; ☺9am-4pm Tue-Fri, 1-5pm Sat & Sun). It may seem a little out of place in a predominately Hispanic town, but it hosts amazingly thoughtful and moving exhibits that are imaginatively presented for maximum impact.

The Drive » Head east on I-10 for two hours, then turn onto TX 118 towards Fort Davis. The area is part of both the Chihuahuan Desert and the Davis Mountains, giving it a unique setting where the endless horizons are suddenly interrupted by rock formations springing from the earth.

TRIP HIGHLIGHT

❷ Fort Davis (p93)

Here's why you'll want to plan on being in Fort Davis on either a Tuesday, Friday or Saturday: to go to an evening star party at

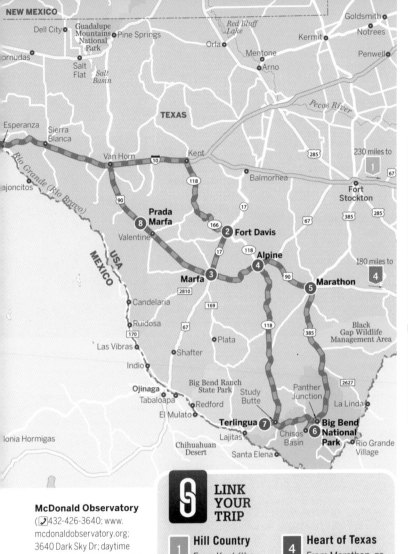

NEW MEXICO

Goldsmith
Dell City
Guadalupe
Mountains
National
Park
Pine Springs
Orla
Kermit
Notrees
ornudas
Penwell
Salt
Flat
Salt
Basin
Mentone
Arno
Red Bluff
Lake

TEXAS

Pecos River

Esperanza
Sierra
Blanca
Van Horn
Kent
285
230 miles to
67
1

Rio Grande (Rio Bravo)
ajoncitos
10
Balmorhea
Fort
Stockton

90
118

285
385
285

**8 Prada
Marfa**
166
2 Fort Davis
17
67

Valentine
17
118
Alpine
4
180 miles to
4

MEXICO

USA

Marfa 3
2810
90
Marathon
5

169

Candelaria

Ruidosa
67
118
385
Black
Gap Wildlife
Management Area

170

Las Vibras
Plata
Shafter
2627

Indio

Ojinaga
Tabaloapa
Big Bend Ranch
State Park
Study
Butte
Panther
Junction
La Linda
Redford

Ionia Hormigas
El Mulato
Terlingua 7
Lajitas
Chisos
Basin
6 **Big Bend
National
Park**
Rio Grande
Village

Chihuahuan
Desert
Santa Elena

McDonald Observatory

(📞432-426-3640; www.
mcdonaldobservatory.org;
3640 Dark Sky Dr; daytime
pass adult/child 6-12yr/under
12yr $8/7/free, star parties
adult/child $12/8; ⏱ visitor
center 10am-5:30pm; 🅿).
The observatory has
some of the clearest and
darkest skies in North
America, not to mention
some of the world's most

🔗 **LINK
YOUR
TRIP**

1 Hill Country
From Kent (the
turnoff for Fort Davis)
continue east on I-10
for 334 miles to join this
loop at Kerrville.

4 Heart of Texas
From Marathon, go
243 miles east on US 90
to catch up with this trip
at Uvalde.

powerful telescopes – a perfect combination for gazing at stars, planets and assorted celestial bodies with astronomers on hand to explain it all.

Other than that, nature lovers will enjoy **Davis Mountains State Park** (p93), and history buffs can immerse themselves at the 1854 **Fort Davis National Historic Site** (p93), a well-preserved frontier military post that's impressively situated at the foot of Sleeping Lion Mountain.

The Drive » Marfa is just 20 minutes south on TX 17, a two-lane country road where tumbleweeds bounce slowly by and congregate around the barbed-wire fences.

TRIP HIGHLIGHT

❸ Marfa (p94)

Marfa got its first taste of fame when Rock Hudson, Elizabeth Taylor

and James Dean came to town to film the 1956 film *Giant*, and has served as a film location for movies like *There Will Be Blood* and *No Country for Old Men*.

But these days, this tiny town with one stoplight draws visitors from around the world for an entirely different reason: its art scene. Donald Judd single-handedly put Marfa on the art-world map in the 1980s when he used a bunch of abandoned military buildings to create one of the world's largest permanent installations of minimalist art at the **Chinati Foundation Museum** (☏432-729-4362; www.chinati.org; 1 Calvary Row; adult/student $25/10; ⏱by guided tour only 10am & 2pm Wed-Sun).

You'll find a variety of art galleries sprinkled around town exploring

everything from photography to sculpture to modern art. **Ballroom Marfa** (☏432-729-3600; www.ballroommarfa.org; 108 E San Antonio; ⏱10am-6pm Wed-Sat, to 3pm Sun) is a great gallery to catch the vibe.

The Drive » Alpine is about half an hour east of Marfa on Hwy 90/67.

❹ Alpine (p95)

The biggest little town in the area, Alpine is the county seat, a college town (Sul Ross State University is here) and the best place to stock up on whatever you need before you head down

WITOLD SKRYPCZAK / GETTY IMAGES ©

MARFA LIGHTS VIEWING AREA

The Marfa Lights that flicker beneath the Chinati Mountains have captured the imagination of many a traveler over the decades; accounts of mysterious lights that appear and disappear on the horizon go all the way back to the 1800s. Numerous studies have been conducted to explain the phenomenon, but the only thing scientists all agree on is that they have no idea what causes the apparition.

Catch the show at the Marfa Lights Viewing Area, on the right side of the road between Marfa and Alpine. From the platform, look south and find the red blinking light (that one's real). Just to the right is where you will (or won't) see the Marfa Lights doing their ghostly thing.

Above: Historic cemetery, Terlingua (p38)

into the Chihuahuan Desert.

Stop by the **Museum of the Big Bend** (p95) to brush up on the history of the Big Bend region. But don't expect it to be dry and dusty. A renovation in 2006 added spiffy new exhibits, and reading is kept to a minimum. Most impressive? The enormous wing bone of the Texas pterosaur found in Big Bend – the largest flying creature ever found, with an estimated wing span of more than 50ft – along with the intimidatingly large re-creation of the whole bird, which is big enough to snatch up a

fully grown human and carry them off for dinner.

The Drive » Keep heading east – half an hour later you'll reach the seriously tiny town of Marathon (pronounced mar-a-thun). The views aren't much during this stretch of the drive, but Big Bend will make up for all that.

– – – – – – – – – – –

❺ Marathon (p96)

This tiny railroad town has two claims to fame: it's the closest town to Big Bend's north entrance, providing a last chance to fill up your car and your stomach. And it's got the **Gage Hotel** (☏432-386-4205; www.gage hotel.com; 102 NW 1st St/Hwy 90), a true Texas treasure

that's worth a peek if not an overnight stay.

The Drive » Heading south on US 385, it's 40 miles to the northern edge of Big Bend, and 40 more to get to the Chisos Basin, the heart of the park. The flat road affords miles and miles of views for most of the drive.

– – – – – – – – – – –

TRIP HIGHLIGHT

❻ Big Bend National Park (p97)

Talk about big. At 1252 sq miles, this national park is almost as big as the state of Rhode Island. Some people duck in for an afternoon, hike a quick trail and head back out, but we recommend staying at least two nights to hit the highlights.

With over 200 miles of trails to explore, it's no wonder hiking is one of the most popular activities, with many of the best hikes leaving from the Chisos Basin. Hit the short, paved **Window View Trail** (0.3 miles) at sunset, then hike the **Window Trail** (4.4 miles) the next morning before it gets too hot. This popular trail has a great payoff: after descending into scrub brush, you enter a shady canyon and scramble around on some rocks, then the trail suddenly ends with a narrowed pass and a 200ft drop-off. Leave from the campground trailhead to shave more than a mile off the hike. The return is steep and unshaded. Spend the afternoon hiking the shady **Lost Mine Trail** (4.8 miles) where the views just get better and better as you climb over 1000ft in elevation; or take a scenic drive to see the eerily abandoned **Sam Nail Ranch** or the scenic **Santa Elena Canyon**.

Another great morning hike is the **Grapevine Hills Trail** (2.2 miles), a desert hike where three acrobatic boulders form a much-photographed, inverted-triangle 'window.'

For riverside hikes, **Rio Grande Village Nature Trail** (0.75 miles) is a good short trail for birding and photography. **Boquillas Canyon Trail** (1.4 miles) has a sandy path to the river, where you can play on the sand slide and enjoy the sunlight dancing on the canyon walls.

The visitor centers have tons of information and great maps. Pick up the *Hiker's Guide to Trails of Big Bend National Park* ($1.95 at park visitor centers) to learn about all your options.

The Drive » From the west park entrance, turn left after 3 miles then follow the signs for Terlingua Ghost Town, just past Terlingua proper. It's about a 45-minute drive from the middle of the park.

TRIP HIGHLIGHT

7 Terlingua (p98)

Quirky Terlingua is a unique combination: it's both a ghost town and a social hub. When the local cinnabar mines closed down in the 1940s, the town dried up and blew away like a tumbleweed, leaving buildings that fell into ruins.

But the area has slowly repopulated, businesses have been built on top of the ruins, and locals gather here for two daily rituals: in the late afternoon, everyone drinks beer on the porch of **Terlingua Trading Company** (p99). And after the sun goes down, the party moves next door to **Starlight Theater** (☎432-371-3400; www.thestarlighttheatre. com; 631 Ivey St; mains $10-21; ⏰5pm-midnight), a restaurant and former movie theater, where there's live music every night.

Come early enough to check out the fascinating **stone ruins** (from the road – they're private property) and the old **cemetery**, which you're welcome to explore.

The Drive » Head north to Alpine, then cut west on US 90. It's a little over five hours back to El Paso, but there's one last stop on your way out that you can't miss.

8 Prada Marfa

So you're driving along a two-lane highway out in the middle of nowhere, when suddenly a small building appears in the distance like a mirage. You glance over and see...a Prada store? Known as the 'Prada Marfa' (although it's really closer to Valentine) this art installation set against the backdrop of dusty west Texas is a tongue-in-cheek commentary on consumerism. You can't go in, but you're encouraged to window shop or snap a photo.

The Drive » Take US 90 back to the I-10 and head west to El Paso.

SAN ANTONIO, AUSTIN & TEXAS BACKCOUNTRY **2** BIG BEND SCENIC LOOP

Right: Rafting on the Rio Grande (p97), Big Bend National Park

MICHAEL MELFORD / GETTY IMAGES ©

Texas Gulf Coast

3

Along more than 400 miles of coastline watch for endangered whooping cranes, explore miles of untouched stretches of sand and revel in great seafood and boozy fun.

TRIP HIGHLIGHTS

190 miles

Aransas National Wildlife Refuge
Spot whooping cranes and other birds

0 miles

Galveston
Beautiful beaches, a rich history and great eating

START
1

●Palacios

Corpus
Christi

3

6

245 miles

Port Aransas
Beach town with mellow vibes and fun bars

FINISH
9 ●Port
Isabel

443 miles

Port Isabel
Old fishing town good for fresh seafood

4 DAYS
443 MILES / 713KM

GREAT FOR...

BEST TIME TO GO
January to June and September to December, when it's not too hot.

 ESSENTIAL PHOTO

A whooping crane at Aransas National Wildlife Refuge.

 BEST FOR BEACHES

From Port Aransas to South Padre Island are miles and miles of white sand.

3 Texas Gulf Coast

The hard white sand forms a sharp contrast to the pure blue of the Gulf of Mexico. Follow this line right round the Texas coast south from the many diversions of Galveston to laid-back beach towns like Port Aransas and South Padre Island where you'll never quite get the sand out of your shorts – or want to. Natural and constructed surprises keep the ride interesting from start to finish.

TRIP HIGHLIGHT

❶ Galveston (p105)
Miles of sugary sand front the Galveston's Gulf Coast seawall. This island is part sunburned beach bum, part genteel Southern lady, with sizable Victorian districts that date to the city's heyday as a port of entry for immigrants heading west. Look into the history of the port and its storm-tossed times at the **Texas Seaport Museum** (www. galvestonhistory.org; cnr

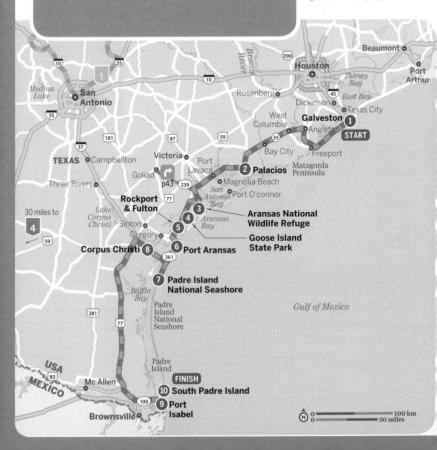

Harborside Dr & 21st St; adult/child $8/5; ⏰10am-4:30pm).

The historic **Strand** commercial district surrounding the Mechanic and 22nd Sts intersection shouldn't be missed. Old-fashioned brick-front buildings are spiffily refurbished, and there are boutiques, ice-cream parlors and general stores filled with curiosities.

The Drive » Cross the San Luis pass bridge to Follets Island. At Surfside Beach, 13.5 miles southeast, go 30 miles inland on TX 332 via Lake Jackson to TX 35. Head south through lush lands laced with rivers for 45 miles.

- - - - - - - - - - - -

 **Palacios**

At a pleasant bend in TX 35, this somewhat frayed small town overlooks an inlet off Matagorda Bay. It's a town with, a realtor would say, a lot of potential, including that found at its small waterfront. Stop into the

LINK YOUR TRIP

4 Heart of Texas
It's 224 miles west of US 77 to Laredo.

1 Hill Country
Head north on I-37 from Corpus Christi to link with this trip in San Antonio.

DETOUR: HISTORIC GOLIAD

Start: ❷ Palacios

'Remember the Alamo!' is the verbal icon of the Texas revolution, but it should also be 'Remember Goliad!' where, on Palm Sunday, March 27, 1836, Mexican general Antonio López de Santa Anna ordered 350 Texian prisoners shot. The death toll was double that of the Battle of the Alamo, and it helped inspire the Texians in their victory over Santa Anna at San Jacinto the following month.

There is a wealth of historic sites in and around the lovely town of Goliad. Start at the 1749 church and fort **Presidio la Bahia** (☎361-645-3752; www.presidiolabahia.org; US 183; adult/child $4/1; ⏰9am-4:45pm). It's 36 miles each way from Tivoli.

once-grand waterfront **Luther Hotel** (☎361-972-2312; www.facebook.com/lutherhotel; 408 S Bay Blvd) and check out the memorabilia from a time when it was an escape for outsized Texas pols like Lyndon Johnson.

The Drive » Continue on TX 35 for 50 miles through Port Lavaca (avoiding any temptation to detour to uninteresting Port O'Connor) until just past tiny Tivoli, where you turn southeast on TX 239. Follow the signs for 18 miles through corn farms until you reach Aransas National Wildlife Refuge.

- - - - - - - - - - - -

TRIP HIGHLIGHT

❸ Aransas National Wildlife Refuge (p107)

Aransas National Wildlife Refuge (www.fws.gov/refuge/aransas; FM 2040; per person/carload $3/5; ⏰6am-dusk, visitor center 8:30am-4:30pm) is a 115,000-acre wetland park that protects the wintering ground of 240 or so whoopers, the most endangered of the planet's cranes. All 500 of the majestic white birds living in the wild or captivity today are descendents of the 15 that remained in the 1940s. Standing nearly 5ft tall, with a 7ft wingspan, whooping cranes are an impressive sight. Easy hiking trails and observation platforms let you spot the birds from November through March.

To get thrilling close-up views from out on the water, take a tour with Captain Tommy's **Rockport Birding & Kayak Adventures** (☎877-892-4737; www.whoopingcranetours.com; 202 N Fulton Beach Rd,

Fulton Habor; 3½hr tours $50; ⊙7:30am & 1pm). His boats are custom-made for whooper-spotting in the shallows outside the refuge. It's not uncommon to spot 60 bird species on a half-day excursion by boat or kayak.

The Drive ❯❯ Take FM 774 through a series of turns 12 miles west to TX 35. Turn south and go 13.5 miles to Lamar and turn east.

❹ Goose Island State Park

The main part of **Goose Island State Park** (☏361-729-2858; www.tpwd. state.tx.us; adult/child $5/ free; ⊙8am-10pm), where admission is charged, is right on Aransas Bay (although there's no swimming). The busiest times at the park are summer and whooping crane season (November to March).

The oldest tree on the coast is an oak in excess of 1000 years old, near the main part of the park. The **'big tree'** (the trunk is more than 35ft in diameter) is in an idyllic spot amid a sea of wildflowers and surrounded by panels with poetry. It's near 12th St and outside of the gated park area.

The Drive ❯❯ It's only 6 miles south on TX 35 to the fun twin coastal towns of Fulton and Rockport.

ROBBIE GEORGE / GETTY IMAGES ©

❺ Rockport & Fulton (p107)

A pedestrian-friendly waterfront, numerous worthy attractions, fishing boats plying their trade and the cute little downtown of Rockport make the adjoining towns of Rockport and Fulton an enjoyable stop.

The side streets between TX 35 and Aransas Bay are dotted with numerous art galleries, especially in the center of Rockport; the towns claim to be home to the state's highest percentage of artists. Commune with crabs and other gulf critters at the small **Aquarium at Rockport Harbor** (p107).

Above: Whooping crane and white-tailed deer, Aransas National Wildlife Refuge (p43)

The Drive » Head 8 miles south on TX 35 to Aransas Pass, turn east on TX 361 for 6.5 miles until you reach the constantly running free ferries for the 10-minute ride to Port Aransas.

- - - - - - - - - - - -

TRIP HIGHLIGHT

⑥ Port Aransas (p108)

Port Aransas (ah-ran-ziss), or Port A, on the northern tip of Mustang Island, is in many ways the most appealing beach town on the Texas coast. It is small enough that you can ride a bike or walk anywhere, but large enough that it has lots of activities and nightlife. The pace is very relaxed, and activities are dominated by hanging out on the beach, fishing and doing nothing. Stop by the **Tarpon Ice House**

(☎361-749-2337; 321 N Allister St; ⊙around 4pm-late), a top local choice for drinking, carousing, mellowing out on the terrace or bursting into song. It's kind of the prototypical beach-town bar.

The Drive » Head south 31 miles on what starts as TX 361 to Padre Island National Seashore. It's all beaches along the way and places like Mustang Island State Park make good stops.

7 Padre Island National Seashore (p110)

If you're looking for more solitude, **Padre Island National Seashore** (www.nps.gov/pais; Park Rd 22; 7-day pass per car $10; ☺visitor center 9am-5pm) fits the bill. Here the tidal flats, shifting dunes and shallow waters provide endless opportunities for hiking, swimming and windsurfing. Most of the 70 miles of this island refuge are accessible by 4WD only along the continuous beach. Hike a mile or two and you'll likely have the place to yourself.

The Drive » Drive 15 miles back north to TX 358 and cross the John F Kennedy Causeway; after another 21 miles you are in the heart of downtown Corpus Christi.

8 Corpus Christi (p110)

In addition to a large marina and strollable waterfront with *miradores* (observation pavilions), the 'City By the Sea' has a small downtown strand and several good museums nearby. Anchored at bay, in front of beach-bum restaurants and T-shirt shops, is the **USS Lexington Museum** (www.usslexington.com; 2914 N Shoreline Blvd; adult/child

$14/9; ☺9am-5pm, to 6pm Jun-Aug). The 900ft naval carrier, the 'Blue Ghost,' is outfitted much as it would have been during its nearly 50 years at sea (it sailed from 1943 to 1991). Explore what's under the waves next door at the **Texas State Aquarium** (☎361-881-1200; www.texasstateaquarium.org; 2710 N Shoreline Blvd; adult/child $18/13; ☺9am-5pm, to 6pm summer; 👪). The jellyfish in the huge tank look ethereal and poetic.

The Drive » Drive 15 miles west to US 77. Turn south and go 30 miles south to Kingsville. Here you can tour the world's largest ranch, King Ranch. Otherwise, continue on US 77 for another 102 miles through dry brushland to TX 100, turn east and drive 24 miles to the coast.

TRIP HIGHLIGHT

9 Port Isabel (p111)

Built in 1852 the atmospheric **lighthouse** (☎956-943-7602; www.portisabelmuseums.com; TX 100 & Tarnava St; adult/child $3/1; ☺9am-5pm) sets the small-town vibe in Port Isabel. The town has the best restaurants in the area and is a delightful place for a waterfront stroll. Fantasize about sunken booty at the **Treasures of the Gulf Museum** (☎956-943-7602; www.portisabelmuseums.com; 317 Railroad Ave; adult/child $3/1; ☺10am-4pm Tue-Sat).

The Drive » A mere 5-mile jaunt over the Queen Isabella Causeway and you're on South Padre Island.

10 South Padre Island (p111)

The town of South Padre Island (SPI) works hard to exploit its sunny climate and beaches. For most of the year utterly mellow bars on the beach and waterfront let you lounge away the day. But for a couple weeks in March SPI becomes a frenetic madhouse during spring break.

Wave-runner rental and parasailing opportunities abound and there are bird-watching trails. You can learn about the slowest moving coastal denizens at **Sea Turtle Inc** (www.seaturtleinc.com; 6617 Padre Blvd; suggested donation adult/child $3/2; ☺10am-4pm Tue-Sun), a rescue facility that offers tours and feeding presentations every half hour. For a drink, try **Boomerang Billy's Beach Bar & Grill** (☎956-761-2420; www.boomerangbillysbeachbar.com; 2612 Gulf Blvd; ☺11am-late), one of the few bars right on the sand on the gulf side. Mellow sounds a bit too energetic for this ultimate crash pad. And as you go north up the 34-mile-long island, the beach becomes ever more quiet and remote.

Right: Texas State Aquarium

Heart of Texas

4

From the Mexican border to the panhandle city of Laredo you'll cross the rural length and breadth of a timeless Texas.

TRIP HIGHLIGHTS

FINISH
Amarillo
Canyon ● ⑨ ──────────── **730 miles**
● Turkey

Palo Duro Canyon State Park
Second only to the Grand Canyon

Big
Spring ●

⑤ ──────────── **355 miles**

San Angelo
Riverside walks, great food and an evocative downtown

275 miles
④

Fort McKavett State Historical Park
Historic, lonely and beautiful

──────────── **0 miles**

Laredo
All the flavor of Mexico north of the border

① **START**

4 DAYS
754 MILES / 1213KM

GREAT FOR...

BEST TIME TO GO

March to June and September to November to avoid scorching heat but enjoy wildflowers.

ESSENTIAL PHOTO

Palo Duro Canyon glowing in a rainbow of colors.

BEST FOR WIDE OPEN SPACES

The view-filling horizon of the plains.

ft: Cotton field, Lubbock (p54)

49

4 Heart of Texas

The big city sprawls of Houston, Dallas and San Antonio seem very far away as you pass through hundreds of miles of open land barely touched by humans. By the time you reach Fort McKavett you may even wonder what century you're in as this old outpost still seems to guard a wild and untamed frontier. At Palo Duro Canyon you'll travel back countless millennia.

TRIP HIGHLIGHT

❶ Laredo (p114)

Even more than other Texas border towns, Laredo has always been tightly entwined with its sister city to the south, the fittingly named Nuevo Laredo.

While the border situation remains unsettled, Laredo's historic old downtown is evocative. Start at leafy **San Agustín Plaza** and stop into the **Republic of the Rio Grande Museum** (☎956-727-3480; www.webbheritage.org; 1005 Zaragoza St; admission $2; ◷9am-4pm Tue-Sat) and grand **San Agustín Church** (San Agustín Plaza; ◷hours vary). Then be sure to spend time at any of the many excellent local restaurants.

The Drive ›› Drive 112 miles north on US 83. The first 60 are through minimalist arid south Texas country, then it becomes more fecund as the road begins to follow rivers and fertile valleys.

---

❷ Uvalde

A pioneer town that was founded in 1853, Uvalde is a busy crossroads with a great **main square** that is crowned by the grand neoclassical 1928 **courthouse**. Stop and stroll the square, pausing for something cool and refreshing along Main St.

The Drive ›› Continue 40 miles north on US 83 through country that rivals the Hill Country in its oak-tree-dotted beauty.

---

❸ Leakey

Since prehistoric times, humans have enjoyed the beauty of the Frio River and its lovely canyon and valley. Tiny Leakey is little more than a crossroads, but what a crossroads! US 83 follows the river north and south, while FM 337 runs east and west through wooded hills and secluded little valleys.

Just 10 miles south of town **Garner State Park** (www.garnerstatepark.com; off US 83) is popular with campers, has kayaking and, since 1941, has had summertime dancing to country tunes playing from a jukebox.

The Drive ›› Go 57 miles north on US 83, then jog west for 18 miles on I-10. Continue north 25 miles on Ranch Rd 1674 through hilly uninhabited land textured with shrubs and trees.

TRIP HIGHLIGHT

❹ Fort McKavett State Historical Park

General William Tecumseh Sherman once called this fort along the San Saba River 'the prettiest post in Texas.' Today, **Fort McKavett State Historical Park** (☎325-396-2358; www.visitfortmckavett.com; FM 864; adult/child $4/3; ◷8am-5pm)

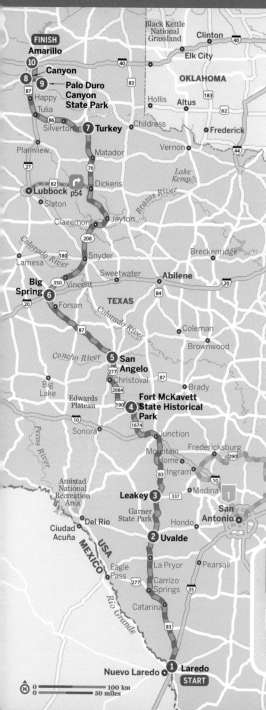

preserves the striking ruins of a once-important fort. It is a beautiful, evocative and remote spot about 75 miles southeast of San Angelo.

Some of the 25 buildings have been restored; the grounds are alive with wildflowers for much of the year. Check out the boiled turnips recipe in the excellent museum.

The Drive » Jog east on FM 864, then head west 17 miles on US 190. Turn north on the wonderfully named Toe Nail Trail/Ranch Rd 2084 (it got its name from the toll it took on the feet of the first soldiers to march the route) and drive 27.5 miles north to US 277, from where San Angelo is another 19 miles north.

TRIP HIGHLIGHT

5 San Angelo (p112)

Situated on the fringes of the Hill Country, San Angelo is the kind of place where nonposer men in suits ride motorcycles, while women in pickups look like they could wrestle a bull and then hit the catwalk. The Concho

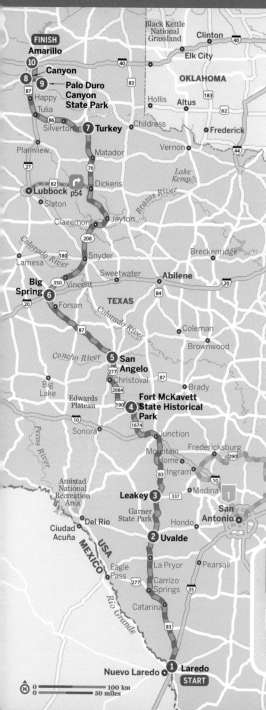

LINK YOUR TRIP

1 Hill Country
Out of Junction, head southwest on the I-10 to link to Kerrville, 54 miles away.

River, which scenically runs through town, offers **walks** along its wild, lush banks.

Fort Concho National Historic Landmark

(📞325-481-2646; www.fortconcho.com; 630 S Oakes St; adult/child $3/1.50; ⏰9am-5pm Mon-Sat, 1-5pm Sun) may be the best-preserved Western frontier fort in the US. Designed to protect settlers and people moving west on the overland trails, the fort went up in 1867 on the fringes of the Texas frontier.

At the heart of not-to-be-missed downtown, the **Concho Avenue Historic District** is a good place to stroll – be sure to pick up a historic walking-tour brochure at the **Visitors Center** (📞325-655-4136, 800-375-1206; www.visitsanangelo.org; 418 W Ave B; ⏰9am-5pm Mon-Sat, noon-4pm Sun). The most interesting section, known as Historic Block One, is between Chadbourne and Oakes Sts. Stop into **Miss Hattie's Bordello Museum** (📞325-653-0112; 18 E Concho Ave; admission free, tours $5; ⏰10am-4pm Tue-Sat, tours 1-4pm Thu-Sat) which operated as a downtown house of pleasure from 1896 until the Texas Rangers shut it down in 1946. Opening hours can be erratic.

At night in San Angelo you can find great food, beer and music.

JEREMY WOODHOUSE / GETTY IMAGES ©

The Drive ≫ Follow the green ribbon of the North Concho River 87 miles northwest on US 87 through lands on the edge of oil country.

----

6 Big Spring (p115)

West of Big Spring, the land is flat and brown for 40 miles to the Permian Basin, where the cities of Midland and Odessa are at the heart of the energy boom. But here, it's quiet and time moves slow. Everywhere that is except at the 15-story **Hotel Settles** (p115), a long-closed 1930s luxury hotel (the product of an oil boom) that reopened in 2013 after a local boy who made good gave it a lavish restoration.

Nearby, 380-acre **Big Spring State Park** (📞432-263-4931; www.tpwd.state.

Above: Bona fide cowboy boots

tx.us; 1 Scenic Dr; admission free; ⊙ dawn to dusk) has a fine nature trail.

There are few west Texas dance halls more authentic than the **Stampede** (☎432-267-2060; 1610 E TX 350), a bare-bones, early-1950s affair 1.5 miles northeast of Big Spring. The schedules, however, are sporadic.

The Drive » Drive 190 miles north through some of the most lonesome terrain in Texas via TX 350, TX 208 and finally TX 70. The latter is a scenic gem, running through towns otherwise bypassed by time. Be sure to keep the tank filled as even some county seats don't have gas stations anymore.

----

❼ Turkey (p118)

Like the flight path of its namesake bird, minute Turkey has been descending for decades.

Bob Wills is one of Texas' most important musicians, and his life is recalled at the modest but worthwhile **Bob Wills Museum** ☎806-423-1146; www.turkeytexas.net; ⊙9-11:30am & 1-4:30pm Mon-Fri, 9am-noon Sat). Located in the old elementary school (which also has the tiny city hall and library), the recently redone displays cover much of Wills'

DETOUR: BUDDY HOLLY'S LUBBOCK

Start: ❻ Big Spring

The hub for the Western music that is emblematic of the Texas plains, Lubbock is the hometown of one of the genre's greatest legends: Buddy Holly. The town celebrates his legacy at the unmissable **Buddy Holly Center** (p115). It's possible to still find the rockabilly sound that Holly made famous in the surrounding **Depot District** at venues like the legendary **Cactus Theater** (p117). Be sure to listen to KDAV AM 1590, which stills plays the music of Holly's era.

See how people lived on the plains over the last 200 years at the excellent **National Ranching Heritage Center** (p115) with dozens of restored old structures in a park-like setting.

From TX 70, Lubbock is 58 miles west on US 82.

---

adventurous life, which included a string of B-movie Westerns. Wills reached his greatest fame in the 1940s with his band the Texas Playboys, with whom he recorded such hits as 'San Antonio Rose' and 'Faded Love'.

The Drive » It's 54 miles of flat Texas two-lane driving west on TX 86. Then turn north, following the train tracks 32 miles north on US 87.

- - - - - - - - - -

❽ Canyon

Georgia O'Keeffe once taught art at the West Texas A&M University in small yet cultured Canyon. Today's campus is home to what many people figure is the best history museum in Texas – the **Panhandle-Plains Historical Museum**

(📞806-651-2244; www.panhandleplains.org; 2401 4th Ave; adult/child $10/5; ⏰9am-6pm Mon-Sat Jun-Aug, to 5pm Sep-May), where the many highlights include a display on the myriad ways to skin a buffalo. You can hit the highlights in an hour or easily lose a day at this Texas plains must-see.

The Drive » The geologic wonders of Palo Duro Canyon are a straight 15 miles east on TX 217.

- - - - - - - - - -

TRIP HIGHLIGHT

❾ Palo Duro Canyon State Park

At 120-miles long and about 5-miles wide, Palo Duro Canyon is second in size only to the Grand Canyon. The cliffs stratified in yellows, reds and oranges, rock towers and other geologic oddities are a refreshing surprise among the seemingly endless flatness of the plains, and are worth at least a gander.

Prehistoric Indians lived in the canyon 12,000 years ago. The more than 26,000 acres that make up the **park** (📞806-488-2227; www.tpwd.state.tx.us; 11450 Park Road 5; adult/child $5/free; ⏰main gate 6am-8pm Mon-Thu, to 10pm Fri & Sat, shorter hours winter) attract hikers, horseback riders and mountain bikers.

The Drive » Retrace your drive 7 miles west on TX 217 and turn due north for 15 miles on FM 1541 N/S Washington St.

- - - - - - - - - -

❿ Amarillo (p120)

Although Amarillo may seem as featureless as the surrounding landscape, there's plenty here to sate even the most attention-challenged. Beef, the big local industry, is at the heart of Amarillo and it features in many of its attractions, including the moo-filled **Amarillo Livestock Auction** (p120).

Don't miss the **San Jacinto District**: the strip between Georgia and Western Sts was once part of Route 66 and is Amarillo's best shopping, dining and entertainment district.

Right: Buddy Holly statue by sculptor Grant Speed, Lubbock (p115)

STEPHEN SAKS / LONELY PLANET / GETTY IMAGES ©

Destinations

San Antonio & Hill Country (p58)

Most of the small towns in the rolling hills and valleys west of Austin and San Antonio are easy day trips from either city.

Big Bend & West Texas (p90)

Explore the expansive Big Bend National Park, and soak up the delicious slowness of west Texas in surprising small towns and ghost-town ruins.

Houston & the Gulf Coast (p100)

Attend world-class museums and award-winning restaurants in Houston before checking out the mellow beach-town scene of Port Aransas and the frenetic hedonism of South Padre Island.

Heart of Texas (p112)

Leave the big smoke behind and you'll find that this may be the part of Texas that most typifies the state to outsiders. This is a land of sprawling cattle ranches, where people still make a living on horseback.

Prickly pear, Big Bend National Park (p97)
DANITA DELIMONT / LONELY PLANET IMAGES ©

San Antonio & Hill Country

Detour down dirt roads in search of fields of wildflowers, check into a dude ranch, float along the Guadalupe River or twirl around the floor of an old dance hall.

So what if the hills are more mole-size than mountainous? They – and the rivers that flow through them – are what define south-central Texas. To the north is the state capital of Austin, where music, music and more music are on the schedule, day and night. Eighty miles south, the major metropolitan center of San Antonio is home to the Alamo and the festive Riverwalk. Between and to the west of the two towns is the Hill Country, where most of the rolling hills and valleys are easy day trips. Here you can eat great barbecue, dance across an old wooden floor or spend a lazy day floating on the river in small Texas-y towns. If you want to get to the heart of Texas in a short time, this is the way to go.

SAN ANTONIO

In most large cities, downtown is bustling with businesspeople dressed for office work hurrying to their meetings and luncheons. Not so in San Antonio. Instead, downtown is filled with tourists in shorts consulting their maps. In fact, many people are surprised to find that two of the state's most popular destinations – the Riverwalk and the Alamo – are right smack-dab in the middle of downtown, surrounded by historic hotels, tourist attractions and souvenir shops. The volume of visitors is daunting, but the lively Tex-Mex culture is worth experiencing.

◉ Sights & Activities

The intersection of Commerce and Losoya Sts is the very heart of downtown and the Riverwalk, which runs in a U-shape below street level. Signs point out access stairways, but a 3D map bought at the info center is the best way to get oriented. The artsy **Southtown** neighborhood and **King William Historic District** lie south along the river.

★ The Alamo   HISTORIC BUILDING
(☑ 210-225-1391; www.thealamo.org; 300 Alamo Plaza; ⊙ 9am-5:30pm Sep-May, to 7pm Jun-Aug) **FREE** Find out why the story of the Alamo can rouse a Texan's sense of state pride like few other things. For many, it's not so much a tourist attraction as a pilgrimage and you might notice some of the visitors getting downright dewy-eyed at the description of how a few hundred revolutionaries died defending the fort against thousands of Mexican troops.

★ Riverwalk   WATERFRONT
(www.thesanantonioriverwalk.com) A little slice of Europe in the heart of downtown San Antonio, the Riverwalk is an essential part of the San Antonio experience. This is no ordinary riverfront, but a charming canal and pedestrian street that is the main artery at the heart of San Antonio's tourism efforts. For the best overview, hop on a Rio San Antonio river cruise.

San Antonio

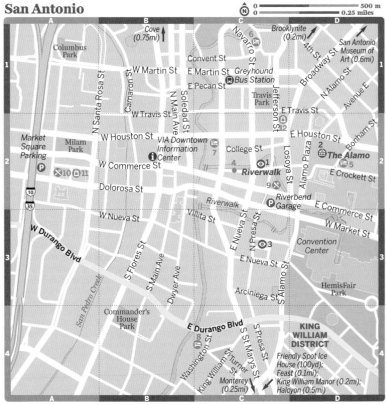

Rio San Antonio Cruises　　　BOAT TOUR
(📞210-244-5700;　　　www.riosanantonio.com;
tour $8.25, taxi one-way/24hr pass from $5/10;
🕘9am-9pm) These 40-minute narrated cruises give you a good visual overview of the
river and a light history lesson. You can buy
your tickets online, or get them on the waterfront at any of the stops. No reservations
are necessary and tours leave every 15 to 20
minutes.

Brackenridge Park　　　PARK
(www.brackenridgepark.org; 3910 N St Mary's St;
miniature train $3.50, carousel $2.50; 🕘5am-11pm)
North of downtown near Trinity University,
this 343-acre park is a great place to spend
the day with your family. In addition to the
San Antonio Zoo (📞210-734-7184; www.sazoo.
org; 3903 N St Mary's St; adult/child $14.25/11.25;
🕘9am-5pm), you'll find the Brackenridge Eagle **miniature train**, an old-fashioned **car-
ousel** and the **Japanese Tea Gardens**.

San Antonio Museum of Art   MUSEUM

(SAMA; www.samuseum.org; 200 W Jones Ave; adult/child $10/free, admission 4-9pm Tue & 10am-noon Sun free; ☺10am-5pm Wed-Sun, to 9pm Tue & Fri) Housed in the original 1880s Lone Star Brewery, which is a piece of art itself, the San Antonio Museum of Art is off Broadway St just north of downtown. San Antonio's strong Latino influence is reflected in an impressive trove of Latin American art, including Spanish Colonial, Mexican and pre-Columbian pieces – it's one of the most comprehensive collections in the US.

McNay Art Museum   MUSEUM

(☑210-824-5368; www.mcnayart.org; 6000 N New Braunfels Ave; adult/child $10/free, special exhibits extra; ☺10am-4pm Tue, Wed & Fri, to 9pm Thu, to 5pm Sat, noon-5pm Sun, grounds 7am-6pm daily) In addition to seeing paintings by household names such as Van Gogh, Picasso, Matisse, Renoir, O'Keeffe and Cézanne, half the fun here is wandering the spectacular Spanish Colonial revival-style mansion, which was the private residence of Marion Koogler McNay.

San Antonio Missions National Historical Park   HISTORIC BUILDING

(www.nps.gov/saan; ☺9am-5pm) Spain's missionary presence can best be felt at the ruins of the four missions south of town: Missions Concepción (1731), San José (1720), San Juan (1731) and Espada (1745–56). Religious services are still held in the mission churches of San José, San Juan and Espada, and the mariachi Mass at 12:30pm on Sunday at San José church is a San Antonio tradition.

★★ Festivals & Events

San Antonio Stock Show & Rodeo   RODEO

(www.sarodeo.com) Big-name concerts follow each night's rodeo; 16 days in mid-February.

Fiesta San Antonio   CULTURAL

(www.fiesta-sa.org) For over 10 days in mid-April there are river parades, carnivals, Tejano music, dancing and tons of food in a mammoth, citywide party.

🛏 Sleeping

San Antonio has a plethora of hotel rooms, so you have plenty of choices right in the downtown area.

★ King William Manor   B&B $$

(☑210-222-0144; www.kingwilliammanor.com; 1037 S Alamo St; d $140-190; P ☻ ✳ 🛜 ✺) In a neighborhood known for beautiful old houses and B&Bs, this grand, Greek Revival mansion occupying a large corner lot still manages to stand out. Maybe it's the columns, maybe it's the sprawling lawn or perhaps the wraparound porches. The inside lives up to the exterior, with understatedly elegant rooms, some of which are enormous.

★ Hotel Havana   HOTEL $$

(☑210-222-2008; www.havanasanantonio.com; 1015 Navarro St; r $115-280; P ☻ ✳ @ 🛜 ✺) Texas design guru and hotelier Liz Lambert could make a radish look cool. Luckily she's turned her sights on fixing up a few lucky properties such as this one, judiciously adding eclectic touches – a retro pink refrigerator, for example – to her clean, elegant designs.

FIESTA SAN ANTONIO

In late April, hundreds of thousands of partygoers throng the streets of San Antonio for Fiesta San Antonio (p105). A 10-day series of riotous events makes for the city's biggest celebration, with general mayhem, fairs, rodeos, races and a whole lot of music and dancing. Going strong after more than 120 years, the festival is the high point of the River City's year.

Fiesta San Antonio dates back to 1891, when local women paraded on horseback in front of the Alamo and threw flowers at each other, all meant to honor the heroes of the Alamo and the Battle of San Jacinto. Today's Battle of the Flowers (www.battleof flowers.org) is only a small piece of Fiesta, which has grown into an enormous party involving 75,000 volunteers, millions of spectators and more than 150 events.

At the beginning of Fiesta week, the Texas Cavaliers' River Parade kicks off with decorated floats drifting along the San Antonio River and a pilgrimage to the Alamo. On the final Saturday night, Fiesta Flambeau claims to be the largest lighted parade in the USA, with marchers carrying candles, sparklers, flashlights, torches and anything else handy.

But locals' top pick of Fiesta week is A Night in Old San Antonio (aka 'NIOSA') which runs for four nights, during which a small army of women volunteers transform La Villita into a multiethnic bazaar of food, music, dancing, arts and much, much more.

GAY & LESBIAN SAN ANTONIO

Despite its conservative outlook, there's definitely a vibrant LGBT community here. In addition to June's PrideFest San Antonio, one of the best times to visit is during Fiesta San Antonio.

➡ The River City's gay nightlife is concentrated along Main and San Pedro Aves, just north of downtown. Venues change, but the strips remain the same.

➡ San Antonio's LGBT Chamber of Commerce (www.sagaychamber.com) provides lists of gay-owned and gay-friendly bars, clubs, businesses and other services.

➡ There's nothing low-key about the Bonham Exchange (www.bonhamexchange.com; 411 Bonham St; ⊘8pm-2am Wed-Sun); this enormous dance club is dark, loud and packed on weekends.

➡ Heat (☑210-227-2600; 1500 N Main Ave; before 11pm free; ⊘4pm-2am Wed-Sat, to midnight Sun), an 18-and-up club, is frequently open after hours and caters to a late-night crowd that comes for the huge dancefloor, techno music, theme nights and drag shows.

Crockett Hotel
HOTEL $$

(☑210-225-6500; www.crocketthotel.com; 320 Bonham St; r $130-180; P✳❄🖧🏊) No wonder pictures of the Alamo are always tightly cropped. Pull back and you can see the Crockett's sign hovering just behind the fort. (In Texas, they call that 'spittin' distance.') Rooms are basic but pleasant enough, and there's an outdoor pool and Jacuzzi, plus a good breakfast buffet.

Noble Inns
B&B $$

(☑210-223-2353; www.nobleinns.com; r from $150; P❄✳🖧🏊) This collection of three inns has something for everyone – at least everyone who likes antiques and Victorian style. Ogé House (209 Washington St; d $150-250, ste $290-370; ✳🖧) is the most elegant of the three, with lushly appointed rooms and a prime location on the residential end of the Riverwalk.

Hotel Valencia
BOUTIQUE HOTEL $$$

(☑210-227-9700; www.hotelvalencia-riverwalk.com; 150 E Houston St; d $170-320; P✳🖧) Faux-mink throws, molded concrete, light shining through perforated metal: this place is all about texture. It could have been transported from New York City – both given its minimalist-chic style and the size of some of the smaller rooms – but it's a hip option for those who eschew chains and historic hotels.

✗ Eating

The Riverwalk offers easy pickings for dinner and drinks, but they're there for the tourists, so don't be surprised if there are busloads of them. South St Marys and S Alamo Sts in the Southtown and King William

districts also host a good number of eateries as does the Pearl Complex, 2 miles north of downtown. Look for hole-in-the-wall Mexican joints scattered the length of N Flores St.

★ Cove
AMERICAN $

(☑210-227-2683; www.thecove.us; 606 W Cypress St; mains $8-12; ⊘11am-10pm Tue-Thu, to 11pm Fri & Sat, noon-8pm Sun; 🖚) This weird, wonderful place is a restaurant, bar, laundromat and car wash. As casual as the restaurant is, the food is top-notch, made from organic, sustainable meat and produce. Sure, it's just tacos, burgers, salads and appetizers but the food is made with love.

Monterey
AMERICAN $$

(☑210-745-2581; www.themontereysa.com; 1127 S St Marys St; mains $9-19; ⊘6-10pm Tue-Thu, to 2am Fri & Sat, 10am-2pm Sun) Extra style points to this King William gastropub located in a former gas station with a big old patio. Despite the small number of options, the menu will please most foodies, and you'll be dazzled by the choices available when it comes to its extensive selection of microbrews and wine. A great all-around place to hang out.

★ Southerleigh
MODERN AMERICAN $$

(☑210-455-5701; www.southerleigh.com; 136 E Grayson St; mains lunch $12-18, dinner $18-36; ⊘11am-midnight Mon-Fri, 2pm-1am Sat; 🖚) In the restaurant-packed Pearl Complex, Southerleigh stands out for its farm-to-table comfort fare. Mac 'n' cheese with crab, cornmeal-crusted catfish, stewed oxtail pie and an enormous gourmet chili dog are recent favorites. The setting is vintage industrial chic: this was once the historical Pearl

Brewery, and excellent and varied house brews (21 on tap) are once again flowing through the 19th-century complex.

Kids get to shape their own pretzels, which are then baked and served as appetizers (free of charge).

Paloma Blanca
MEXICAN **$$**

(210-822-6151; 5800 Broadway St, Alamo Heights; mains lunch $8-11, dinner $10-25; 11am-9pm Mon-Wed, to 10pm Thu & Fri, 10am-10pm Sat, 10am-9pm Sun) There are oodles of great Mexican choices around, but this place sets itself apart with a sleek and stylish ambience – think dim lighting, exposed brick walls and oversize artwork – and outstanding traditional cooking (enchiladas, chiles rellenos, quesadillas).

Mi Tierra Cafe & Bakery
TEX-MEX **$$**

(210-225-1262; www.mitierracafe.com; 218 Produce Row; mains $12-18; 24hr) Dishing out traditional Mexican food since 1941, this 500-seat behemoth in Market Square sprawls across several festively decorated dining areas, giving the busy waitstaff and strolling mariachis quite a workout. It's also open 24 hours, making it ideal for 3am enchilada cravings.

Feast
TAPAS **$$**

(210-354-1024; www.feastsa.com; 1024 S Alamo St; small plates $7-22, brunch $10-16; 5-10pm Tue-Thu, to 11pm Fri & Sat, 10:30am-2:30pm Sun) The seasonally inspired tapas dishes are solid, but the atmosphere alone is worth the trip to King William district. Clear Lucite chairs, sparkly pendant lights and faux taxidermy come together to provide a whimsically modern feel. The front patio is even more enticing, with twinkling lights beneath a big, shady tree and a gardenlike backdrop.

Boudro's
TEX-MEX **$$$**

(210-224-8484; 421 E Commerce St, Riverwalk; mains lunch $11-16, dinner $24-38; 11am-11pm Sun-Thu, to midnight Fri & Sat) This brightly colored waterside restaurant is hugely popular with locals. Fresh guacamole is made right at your table. The upscale Tex-Mex menu reveals some gourmet surprises, such as jumbo shrimp and gulf crab enchiladas, mesquite-grilled quail stuffed with wild mushrooms, and achiote-spiced lamb chops.

Drinking & Nightlife

The Riverwalk's many chain clubs blur together even before you've started drinking. Resist their glossy allure and opt for one of these San Antonio originals.

★ Friendly Spot Ice House
BAR

(210-224-2337; 943 S Alamo St; 3pm-midnight Mon-Fri, from 11am Sat & Sun;) What could be friendlier than a big, pecan-tree-shaded yard filled with colorful metal lawn chairs? Friends (and their dogs) gather to knock back some longnecks while the kids amuse themselves in the playground area.

ROMEO BANIAS / GETTY IMAGES ©

Swimming and tubing on the San Marcos River (p82)

Brooklynite COCKTAIL BAR
(📞 212-444-0707; www.thebrooklynitesa.com; 516 Brooklyn Ave; ⊙5pm-2am) Beer and wine are easy to come by in San Antonio, but this is where you head for a creative, handcrafted cocktail. Vintage wallpaper and wingback chairs give the place a dark, Victorian-esque decor: sip a mezcal-topped Doxycycline or the bourbon-forward Lion's Tail in a fittingly dignified atmosphere.

Cove BEER HALL
(📞 210-227-2683; www.thecove.us; 606 W Cypress St; ⊙11am-10pm Tue-Thu, to 11pm Fri & Sat, noon-8pm Sun; 🔊) Live music is just part of the reason to hang out at this chill beer hall. The Cove is a unique combo of food stand, cafe, laundromat and car wash. It even has a kiddie playground.

Halcyon CAFE
(www.halcyoncoffeebar.com; 1414 S Alamo St; ⊙7am-2am Mon-Fri, from 8am Sat & Sun; 📶) With excellent coffees, creative cocktails and an inviting coffeehouse vibe (with outdoor seating as well), Halcyon makes a fine destination after a bike ride along the river. There's plenty of good snacking and dining choices, and even make-your-own s'mores for the pyrotechnically inclined. Occasional live music.

⭐ Entertainment

For listings of local music and cultural events, pick up the free weekly *San Antonio Current* (www.sacurrent.com).

Four-time NBA champions the **San Antonio Spurs** (www.nba.com/spurs) shoot hoops at the **AT&T Center** (📞tickets 800-745-3000; www.attcenter.com; 1 AT&T Center Pkwy) off I-35. Purchase tickets through **Ticketmaster** (www.ticketmaster.com).

🛍 Shopping

A few artisan craft shops exist among the tourist-T-shirt-filled Riverwalk. The old buildings of the city's first neighborhood, **La Villita Historic Arts Village** (📞210-207-8614; www.lavillita.com; 418 Villita St; ⊙most shops 10am-6pm), house the largest concentration of galleries and boutiques.

Pearl Complex MALL
(www.atpearl.com; 200 E Grayson St) The old Pearl Brewery has received a massive face-lift as part of the new Pearl development north of downtown, including shops, cafes and restaurants.

WORTH A TRIP

FLOORE'S COUNTRY STORE

This terrific old bar and dance hall first opened in 1942 as a store run by a friend of Willie Nelson. (Willie used to play here nightly; the sign still says so.) Visit **John T Floore's Country Store** (📞210-695-8827; www.liveatfloores.com; 14492 Old Bandera Rd, Helotes; ⊙11am-midnight Fri & Sat, to 10pm Sun) today and you'll discover the true way to hear Texas country music, whether in the outdoor yard or by the fire in the rustic building. There are performances on Friday and Saturday nights; Sunday night is family dance night and there's no cover. Bandera Rd is off Hwy 16.

Market Square MARKET
(📞 210-207-8600; www.marketsquaresa.com; 514 W Commerce St; ⊙10am-8pm Jun-Aug, to 6pm Sep-May) A little bit of Mexico in downtown San Antonio, Market Square is a fair approximation of a trip south of the border, with Mexican food, mariachi bands and store after store filled with Mexican wares. A big chunk of the square is taken up by El Mercado, the largest Mexican marketplace outside of Mexico.

Paris Hatters ACCESSORIES
(📞 210-223-3453; www.parishatters.com; 119 Broadway St; ⊙10:30am-6:30pm Mon-Sat, noon-5pm Sun) Despite the name, this is no Parisian haberdashery, but a purveyor of fine cowboy hats established in 1917. You'll walk out looking like a real cowboy with a hat that's been shaped and fitted to your very own noggin. It's one of the best places in the state to get a Stetson (or whatever brand of hat is mutually agreed to suit you).

ℹ️ Information

Visitor center 'amigos' (in turquoise shirts and straw hats) roam the downtown core offering directions.

Convention & Visitors Bureau (📞800-447-3372; www.visitsanantonio.com; 317 Alamo Plaza; ⊙9am-5pm, to 6pm Jun-Aug) Stop by the well-stocked Convention & Visitors Bureau, opposite the Alamo, for maps and brochures; their website also has loads of information useful for preplanning. The staff can answer any questions you have and can also sell you passes for tours or for VIA buses and streetcars.

San Antonio Public Library (www.mysapl.org; 600 Soledad St; ⊙9am-9pm Mon-Thu, to 5pm

Fri & Sat, 11am-5pm Sun) Branch locations provide free internet access across the city.

⊙ Getting There & Around

San Antonio is served by the **San Antonio International Airport** (SAT; ☑ 210-207-3433; www.sanantonio.gov/sat; 9800 Airport Blvd), about 9 miles north of downtown. **VIA Metropolitan Transit** (☑ 210-362-2020; www.viainfo.net; ride/day pass $1.20/4) city bus 2 runs from the airport to downtown. A taxicab ride will cost about $26. Major car-rental agencies all have offices at the airport.

The free tourist-friendly E trolleybus runs a circular route around downtown. Loads of buses go further afield. Buy a day pass ($4) at the **VIA Downtown Information Center** (☑ 210-362-2020; www.viainfo.net; 211 W Commerce St; ⊙ 7am-6pm Mon-Fri, 9am-2pm Sat).

You can also get around town by checking out a bike from one of the many kiosks of **San Antonio B-cycle** (sanantonio.bcycle.com).

HILL COUNTRY

New York has the Hamptons, San Francisco has the wine country, and Texas has the Hill Country. Just an hour or two's drive from both Austin and San Antonio, the area is an easy day trip or weekend getaway, and its natural beauty paired with the locals' easygoing nature has inspired more than a few early retirements.

Thanks to former First Lady Claudia Taylor Johnson – 'round here everyone calls her Lady Bird – each spring the highways are lined with eye-popping wildflowers that stretch for miles and miles, planted as part of her Highway Beautification Act.

In addition to boasting the bluebonnets, Indian paintbrushes and black-eyed Susans that blanket the roads, the Hill Country contests Texas' reputation as being dry and flat, with rolling hills, giant oak trees, spring-fed creeks and flowing rivers.

HILL COUNTRY WINERIES

When most people think of Texas, they think of cowboys, cacti and Cadillacs – not grapes. But the Lone Star State has become the fifth-largest wine-producing state in the country (behind California, Washington, New York and Oregon). The Hill Country, with its robust Provence-like limestone and hot South African–style climate, has become the most productive wine-making region in the state, and these rolling hills are home to more than a dozen wineries. The largest concentration of vineyards is around Fredericksburg.

Most wineries are open daily for tastings and tours. Many also host special events, such as grape stompings and annual wine and food feasts. Local visitors bureaus stock the handy *Texas Hill Country Wine Trail* leaflet, which details the wineries and schedules of wine-trail weekends (or visit www.texaswinetrail.com). You could leave the driving to someone else with Texas Wine Tours (☑ 830-997-8687; www.texas-wine-tours.com; tours per person $109-219), which run tours in a limousine-style bus, or Fredericksburg Limo & Wine Tours (limo tours $99-149, shuttle bus tours $89-139), which offer limo tours or more affordable shuttle van tours. Hill Country wineries to check out include the following.

Becker Vineyards (☑ 830-644-2681; www.beckervineyards.com; 464 Becker Farms Rd; ⊙ 10am-5pm Mon-Thu, to 6pm Fri-Sat, noon-6pm Sun) Located 10 miles east of Fredericksburg, just off US 290, this is one of the state's most decorated wine producers. Its vineyard has 36 acres of vines and allegedly Texas' largest underground wine cellar. Its tasting room is housed in a beautiful old stone barn.

Fall Creek Vineyards (☑ 325-379-5361; www.fcv.com; 1820 CR 222; ⊙ 11am-5pm Mon-Sat, noon-4pm Sun) This well-known vineyard is located just over 2 miles north of the post office in the town of Tow, close to Llano, and is perched beautifully on the shores of Lake Buchanan. Fall Creek churns out several different French- and German-style varietals, including a popular chenin blanc and a tasty Riesling. The winery offers a colorful, modern tasting room as well.

Dry Comal Creek Winery & Vineyards (☑ 830-885-4076; www.drycomalcreek.com; 1741 Herbelin Rd, off Hwy 46; ⊙ noon-5pm daily) A smaller vineyard with wines that have begun to turn heads is the unique Dry Comal Creek Winery & Vineyards, located about 7 miles west of New Braunfels. Proprietor Franklin Houser gives his own tours around the tiny winery, which is constructed of stone and cedar wood.

THE HOME OF SHINER BOCK

The highlight of any trip to Shiner, TX, the self-proclaimed 'cleanest little city in Texas,' is a tour of the **Spoetzl Brewery** (☑361-594-3852; www.shiner.com; 603 E Brewery St; tours free; ⊙tours 11am & 1:30pm Mon-Fri year-round, plus 10am & 2:30pm Jun-Aug) **FREE** where Shiner Bock beer is brewed. Czech and German settlers who began making beer under brewmaster Kosmos Spoetzl founded the brewery 100 years ago. Today the brewery still produces several types using the same methods, including bock, blonde, honey wheat, summer stock and winter ale. You can sample the beers for free after the tour in the little bar.

Shiner is about an hour and a half (92 miles) east of San Antonio by car; to get there, take I-10 east 57 miles, head south on US 183, then east on US 90 at Gonzales. It's about the same distance from Austin; just take US 183 south and follow the same directions starting at Gonzales.

❶ Orientation

Ask 10 people the boundaries of the Hill Country and you'll get 11 different answers but, generally speaking, the Hill Country is an area west of the I-35 corridor between Austin and San Antonio, with Fredericksburg and Kerrville being the westernmost points and largest towns. Some people consider San Marcos, New Braunfels and Gruene to be part of the Hill Country, but you really have to leave the interstate to get the effect.

❶ Information

You can spend an entire vacation in the Hill Country and not see it all. The best time to visit is spring when temperatures are mild and the wildflowers are in full bloom, but many people also enjoy visiting in December when the towns light up for the holiday season. Visit www.hill-country-visitor.com for information on special events, accommodations, outdoor recreation and other Hill Country destinations.

Boerne

POP 10,884

Twenty-three miles east of Bandera on Hwy 46 is the bustling little center of Boerne (pronounced 'Bernie'), settled by German immigrants in 1849. The town, which clings strongly to its German roots, is less overrun with tourists than Fredericksburg and is a pleasant place to spend a few hours.

The **Boerne Convention & Visitors Bureau** (☑830-249-7277; www.visitboerne.org; 1407 S Main St; ⊙9am-5pm Mon-Fri, to noon Sat) has tons of information about the town and surrounding area. Main St seems to focus on antique stores; most stock a handy leaflet that will help you navigate the plethora of shops.

◉ Sights & Activities

Cibolo Nature Center   OUTDOORS
(☑830-249-4616; www.cibolo.org; 140 City Park Rd, off Hwy 46; ⊙8am-dusk) East of Main St, this small park has rewarding nature trails that wind through native Texan woods, marshland and along Cibolo Creek. Call the park visitor center to ask about the series of live-music concerts and events held here during summer.

Cascade Caverns   CAVE
(☑830-755-8080; www.cascadecaverns.com; 226 Cascade Caverns Rd, off I-10 exit 543; adult/child 4-11yr $15/9.50) Natural attractions outside town include popular Cascade Caverns, about 3 miles south of Boerne. The caverns include a 140ft-deep cave that features giant stalagmites and stalactites and a 100ft waterfall, which you can see by taking the one-hour tour. Opening hours vary, so check the website for details.

🛏 Sleeping & Eating

Ye Kendall Inn   HISTORIC HOTEL $$
(☑800-364-2138; www.yekendallinn.com; 128 W Blanco Rd; d $100-200, cabins $109-249; ❶) A national-landmark hotel dating from 1859, this is the nicest place to stay in Boerne. The creekside main house is made of hand-cut limestone and features a two-story, 200ft-long front porch. The hotel also has three cabins and a small church, all of which date from the 1800s and were relocated to the property from various sites around the state (the stunning Enchanted Cabin was built near Enchanted Rock).

Bear Moon Bakery & Cafe
CAFE **$**

(☏830-816-2327; 401 S Main St; mains $4-11; ☺6am-5pm Tue-Sat, 8am-4pm Sun) For a fresh, delicious breakfast buffet, don't look any further than Bear Moon Bakery & Cafe. On weekends, be sure to arrive early – it's always packed. There are plenty of home-baked goodies to tempt you, along with fresh soups, salads and sandwiches for lunch.

Daily Grind
CAFE **$**

(☏830-249-4677; 143 S Main St; ☺7am-6pm Mon-Fri, 8am-6pm Sat, 9am-5pm Sun) A prime choice for early-morning coffee and tea is this cute little spot right on the main strip.

Dodging Duck Brewhaus
BREWPUB **$$**

(☏830-248-3825; www.dodgingduck.com; 402 River Rd; mains $9-17; ☺11am-9pm Mon-Thu, to 10pm Fri-Sun) Offers a tasty mix of Mexican and German fare, and homemade beers, in an eclectic atmosphere. In addition to lunch and dinner, it also has plenty of shareable bar snacks.

Po Po Family Restaurant
AMERICAN **$$**

(☏830-537-4194; 829 FM 289; mains $10-40; ☺11am-8:30pm Sun-Thu, to 9:30pm Fri & Sat) Out on the edge of town, this restaurant serves steaks and seafood – including hard-to-find frog legs – but the main reason to come here is to see the absolutely astounding collection of souvenir plates: more than 2000 of them cover almost every inch of wall space.

Bandera

POP 864

It's not always easy finding real, live cowboys in Texas, but it is in Bandera, which has branded itself the Cowboy Capital of Texas. During the summer there are usually rodeos every weekend, and on Saturday afternoons gunslingers and cowboys roam the streets and entertain the crowds during Cowboys on Main. Check the Bandera County Convention & Visitors Bureau (CVB; ☏800-364-3833; www.banderacowboycapital.com; 126 Hwy 16; ☺9am-5pm Mon-Fri, 10am-3pm Sat) website for the exact schedules and locations.

Ready to saddle up? The friendly folks at the visitors bureau also know nearly a dozen places in and around town where you can go horseback riding. For overnights, they can direct you to dude ranch accommodations, with packages that include lodging, meals and an equine excursion; plan on spending about $130 to $160 per adult per night ($45 to $90 for the young'uns).

Another great reason to come to Bandera? Drinking beer and dancing in one of the many hole-in-the-wall cowboy bars or honky-tonks, where you'll find friendly locals, good live music and a rich atmosphere. Mosey over to the patio at 11th Street Cowboy Bar (www.11thstreetcowboybar.com; 307 11th St; ☺10am-2am Tue-Sat, from noon Sun) or Arky Blue's Silver Dollar Saloon (308 Main St; ☺10am-2am). Both bars have live country crooners from Friday to Sunday.

Comfort

POP 2363

For some true historic charm, spend the night at Hotel Faust (☏830-995-3030; www.hotelfaust.com; 717 High St; d $110-160, 2-bedroom cottage $175-195; ☺✱). The limestone building dates from the late 1800s, but the rooms have all been gutted and beautifully restored. For a special treat, stay in their Ingenhuett Log Cabin, built in the 1820s and moved to its present location from Kentucky.

The nicest restaurant in town is 814: A Texas Bistro (☏830-995-4990; www.814atexasbistro.com; 713 High St; dinner $23-30; ☺6-9pm Thu & Fri, 11:30am-2pm & 6-9pm Sat, 11:30am-2pm Sun). Located in the former Comfort post office and sporting a rustic decor, this place is pure Hill Country. There's not a huge array of choices – dinner has three mains options that change weekly – so the focus is

Windmill, Kerrville
BILL HEINSOHN / ALAMY STOCK PHOTO ©

LOST MAPLES STATE NATURAL AREA

The foliage spectacle in October and November at Lost Maples State Natural Area (☑830-966-3413, reservations 512-389-8900; www.tpwd.state.tx.us; 37221 RR 187, 5 miles north of Vanderpool; day use $3-6, primitive camping $10, tent sites $20) is as colorful as any you'd see in New England. In autumn bigtooth maple trees turn shocking golds, reds, yellows and oranges. In the summertime there's good swimming in the Sabinal River. At any time of the year, campers will find backcountry primitive areas where they can pitch a tent, as well as more convenient sites supplied with water, electricity and nearby showers. Hiking trails will take visitors into rugged limestone canyons and prairielike grasslands populated by bobcats, peccaries and gray foxes. Bird-watching is another popular attraction at Lost Maples because of the green kingfishers, who take up residence in the park year-round.

on doing just a couple of things but doing them really well.

For something more casual, you can't beat Comfort Pizza (☑830-995-5959; 802 High St; whole pizza $15-20; ⊙11am-10pm Mon-Sun). Creative ingredient combos make choosing your pizza fun: the prosciutto, pineapple and serrano chili pizza, for example, is known as the Angry Samoan. Enjoy a glass of wine or a prickly-pear-cactus drink on the colorful patio filled with big metal lawn chairs.

Comfort is about halfway between Kerrville and Boerne on TX 27, just 2 miles west of I-10.

Kerrville

POP 22,373

If Fredericksburg feels too fussy for you, Kerrville also makes a good base for exploring the Hill Country. It's home to one of the world's best museums of cowboy life and a jam-packed springtime folk festival. It may not turn on the charm, but it's also a welcome relief for anyone suffering quaintness overload.

☉ Sights

Kerr Arts & Cultural Center   ARTS CENTER
(☑830-895-2911; www.kacckerrville.com; 228 Earl Garrett St; ⊙10am-4pm Tue-Sat, from 1pm Sun) FREE Catch the pulse of the Hill Country art scene here. Located in the old post office, it frequently changes exhibits, which could include anything from quilts to watercolors to gourd art.

Schreiner Mansion   HISTORIC BUILDING
(☑830-896-8633; 226 Earl Garrett St; ⊙11am-4pm Tue-Sat) FREE Check out the opulent former residence of Charles Schreiner (the

man who built half the town). The exterior stonework is impressive; if you like historic homes, head inside to see more.

Museum of Western Art   MUSEUM
(☑830-896-2553; www.museumofwesternart.com; 1550 Bandera Hwy; adult/student/under 8yr $7/5/free; ⊙10am-4pm Tue-Sat) This is a nonprofit showcase of Western Americana. The quality and detail of the work, mostly paintings and bronze sculptures, is astounding; all depict scenes of cowboy life, the Western landscape or vignettes of Native American life.

The museum has permanent displays of two artists' studios, the equipment of cowboy life (where kids can climb on saddles, feel a lasso and play with spurs), and a research library available to anyone interested in learning more about the frontier.

🏃 Activities

The Guadalupe River runs through Kerrville, and there are lots of different ways to enjoy it.

Kerrville-Schreiner Park   PARK
See p25.

Louise Hays City Park   PARK
(202 Thompson Dr; ⊙dawn-11pm) At 60 acres it's smaller than Kerrville-Schreiner but, on the plus side, it's free. Enjoy river access, shaded picnic tables, sports courts and barbecue pits.

Guadalupe Street City Park   PARK
(1001 Junction Hwy; ⊙7:30am-11pm) Take a refreshing swim in the river at this spot, behind the Inn of the Hills Resort. The water here is deep and not recommended for children.

Riverside Nature Center PARK

(📞830-257-4837; 150 Francisco Lemos St; ☺dawn-dusk) Near the river, at the south end of downtown, this center has walking trails, a wildflower meadow and Guadalupe River access.

Kerrville Kayak & Canoe Rentals KAYAKING

(📞830-895-4348; www.paddlekerrville.com; 130 W Main St; per hr $10-15) Rents watercraft by the hour from Kerrville-Schreiner Park. You can save money with half-day or full-day rentals, and also by picking up your craft from the shop.

Festivals & Events

Kerrville Folk Festival MUSIC

(📞830-257-3600; www.kerrville-music.com; 3876 Medina Hwy) The Quiet Valley Ranch turns up the volume each spring. This 18-day musical extravaganza starts right around Memorial Day and features music by national touring acts and local musicians. One-day tickets cost $25 to $40; check the website for information about camping at the ranch.

Kerrville Wine & Music Festival MUSIC

(☺Labor Day weekend) A four-day miniversion of the folk festival.

Sleeping

If you're planning on heading to Kerrville during any of the festivals, book months in advance. Kerrville doesn't have the glut of charming B&Bs you'll find in Fredericksburg; the lodgings here cater to practical travelers. There are several chains right off the highway

---

WHAT THE...? STONEHENGE II

So Stonehenge II isn't the real Stonehenge. We're not real druids, so there you go. This second-string henge has much less mysterious origins than the ancient megalithic structure near Salisbury, England. Two locals built the 60% scale model out of concrete and threw in some Easter Island statues for good measure.

Just a few years back you could find it out in a field on a country road, but alas, the property changed hands and the new owners weren't interested in maintaining the henge's important cultural legacy. Luckily, the installation has been saved by the Hill Country Arts Foundation (120 Point Theatre Road S, Ingram), whose lawn it now graces.

---

on Sidney Baker St. They're interchangeable, but they're there if you need them.

★Inn of the Hills Resort
& Conference Center MOTEL $

(📞830-895-5000, 800-292-5690; www.innofthehills.com; 1001 Junction Hwy; d $77-104; ☺ ✳ 🛜 🏊) The renovated rooms that open onto the pool are a lovely surprise; they were among the nicest we saw in town. However, the unrenovated rooms have a lot of catching up to do, so make sure you know what you're getting when you book.

The common areas are nice enough, although the restaurant is a little countrified. The best feature of all is the beautiful Olympic-style pool surrounded by shade trees.

Kerrville-Schreiner Park CAMPGROUND $

(📞830-257-5392; 2385 Bandera Hwy; day-use per person $4, campsites $10-20, RV sites $23-28; 🏊) This is a beautiful park set right on the river. Pitch a tent or hook up your RV in one of the well-tended campsites, then go enjoy the 500 acres.

YO Ranch Resort Hotel HOTEL $$

(📞830-257-4440, 877-967-3767; www.yoresort.com; 2033 Sidney Baker St; r from $79, ste from $185; ✳ 🛜 🏊 🐾) If you're one of those folks who's freaked out by taxidermy, you might want to mosey on past. If you're not, this is one of the more interesting hotel lobbies you'll see, lined with trophy mounts of elk, moose and longhorns, plus a large, stuffed grizzly bear.

Oh, you wanted to know about the rooms as well? They're on the bland side, but who needs 'em: the resort also has court facilities for tennis, basketball and volleyball, a walking track and a playground.

Trail's End Guesthouse B&B $$

(📞830-377-1725; www.trailsendguesthouse.com; 180 Gay Dr N; d $99-139; ☺ 🛜 🐾) East of town, this guesthouse has a rustic charm that fits right into the surrounding hills, with exposed beams and plank walls in every room and cabin. Did we mention a hearty breakfast is delivered right to your door?

Eating

★Taco To Go MEXICAN $

(📞830-896-8226; 428 Sidney Baker St; tacos $2; ☺6am-9pm Mon-Sat, 7am-2pm Sun) You can take your tacos to go or eat inside, but don't miss out on the excellent soft tacos – including breakfast tacos served all day – made with homemade tortillas and salsa.

YO RANCH

Texas is full of ranches, but not many of those ranches are full of exotic game. Established in 1880 by Kerrville merchant Charles Schreiner, the YO Ranch (✆830-640-3222; www.yoranch.com; 1736 YO RR, Mountain Home) once encompassed 600,000 acres. It was Charles Schreiner III who started a wildlife conservation program in the 1960s, and these days you can find up to 55 species of exotic animals roaming the ranch, from gazelles to wildebeests to the beautiful scimitar-horned oryx.

The best way to experience the ranch is on a wildlife tour, where you'll be loaded on a bus and taken up close enough to get some pretty great pictures. And not to spoil any surprises, but at the end you might just get to feed a giraffe (bring wet wipes; they're slobbery). The regular two-hour tour ($35) is offered Thursday through Sunday and includes a chuck-wagon lunch. If that's just not enough time, you can go all out and book a five-hour photo safari ($250).

The ranch also offers horseback rides (per first hour $45, per each additional hour $35) and overnight visits. The ranch also runs hunting tours, which do take place away from the wildlife tours.

Hill Country Cafe
CAFE $

(✆830-257-6665; www.hill-country-cafe.com; 806 Main St; menu items $2-10; ⊘6am-2pm Mon-Fri, 6-11am Sat) This tiny hole-in-the-wall diner near the historic district serves up hearty home cooking in heaping portions, including just about everything you could want for breakfast as well as sandwiches and lunch plates.

Conchita's Mexican Cafe
MEXICAN $

(✆830-895-7708; 810 Main St; mains $8-11; ⊘11am-3pm Mon-Fri, from 10am Sat & Sun) Located in an unassuming storefront on Main St, Conchita's doesn't look like much, but the inventive dishes such as Mexican egg rolls really stand out from typical Mexican fare.

Classics Burgers & 'Moore'
BURGERS $

(✆830-257-8866; 448 Sidney Baker St; mains $7-11; ⊘11am-3pm & 5-8pm Mon-Fri, 11am-3pm Sat) This burger joint does have sort of a classic quality to it, and its burgers and fries blow the fast-food-chain offerings out of the water.

★ Grape Juice
AMERICAN $$

(✆830-792-9463; www.grapejuiceonline.com; 623 Water St; mains $10-15; ⊘11am-11pm Tue-Sat) For us, it was love at first sight – the sight being a little menu item called the Honey Badger that's a ridiculously wonderful combination of 'crack'-aroni and cheese surrounded by a moat of chili with Fritos on top. It's a somewhat undignified dish considering the lovely wine-bar atmosphere, which is exactly what we love about it.

La Four's Seafood Restaurant
SEAFOOD $$

(✆830-896-1449; 1705 Junction Hwy; mains $12-22; ⊘11am-2pm & 4-9pm Tue-Sat, 11am-2:30pm Sun) Head to this riverside spot that looks like a big tin shed for excellent fried shrimp and Cajun-influenced fare such as frog legs and spicy jalapeño hush puppies.

Rails Cafe at the Depot
AMERICAN $$

(✆830-257-3877; www.railscafe.com; 615 E Schreiner; meals $9-19; ⊘11am-9pm Mon-Sat) This cute cafe in the old train depot is awfully pleasant. Make a lunch of panini or salad, or splurge a bit with the osso bucco or beef tenderloin.

Francisco's
AMERICAN $$

(✆830-257-2995; www.franciscos-restaurant.com; 201 Earl Garrett St; lunch $7-10, dinner $13-38; ⊘11am-3pm Mon-Wed, 11am-3pm & 5:30-9pm Thu-Sat) Colorful, bright and airy, this bistro and sidewalk cafe is housed in an old limestone building in the historic district. It's packed at lunch, and is one of the swankiest places in town for a weekend dinner.

❶ Information

Kerrville's excellent **visitor center** (✆830-792-3535, 800-221-7958; www.kerrvilletexascvb.com; 2108 Sidney Baker St; ⊘8:30am-5pm Mon-Fri, 9am-3pm Sat, 10am-3pm Sun) has everything you'll need to get out and about in the Hill Country, including heaps of brochures and coupon books for accommodations.

The **Butt-Holdsworth Memorial Library** (✆830-257-8422; 505 Water St; ⊘10am-6pm Mon, Wed, Fri & Sat, to 8pm Tue & Thu, 1-5pm Sun) provides free internet access. You can change money at **Bank of America** (✆830-792-0430;

601 Main St; ⊙9am-4pm Mon-Thu, to 5pm Fri, 9am-noon Sat), which also has an ATM. **Peterson Regional Medical Center** (☑830-896-4200; www.petersonrmc.com; 551 Hill Country Dr) has a new facility and 24-hour emergency services.

ℹ Getting There & Around

Kerrville is half an hour south of Fredericksburg on Hwy 16, or just over an hour northwest from San Antonio on I-10. In town, Hwy 16 becomes Sidney Baker St, and Hwy 27 (aka Junction Hwy) becomes Main St.

From Austin, take US 290 west to Fredericksburg, then turn south onto Hwy 16, which meets Kerrville south of I-10. From San Antonio, take I-10 north to Hwy 16, then head south.

In town, **Bicycle Works** (☑830-896-6864; www.hillcountrybicycle.com; 141 W Water St; full-day rental $28; ⊙10am-6pm Mon-Fri, to 4pm Sat) rents bikes.

Fredericksburg

POP 10,890

With fields full of wildflowers, shops full of antiques, and streets full of historic buildings and B&Bs, Fredericksburg is the poster child for 'quaint,' serving as the region's largest old German-settled town (c 1870) and unofficial capital of the Hill Country.

It's more cute than cool, but it's not a bad place to linger a bit – especially during wildflower season. It also makes a good base of operations for exploring the surrounding areas. Stop by the Fredericksburg Visitor Information Center (☑830-997-6523, 888-997-3600; www.visitfredericksburgtx.com; 302 E Austin St; ⊙9am-5pm Mon-Sat, 11am-3pm Sun; 🛜) to get your bearings.

◉ Sights & Activities

Spend an hour or two wandering the town's historic district; despite having more than

---

URBAN PLANNING

Street names in Fredericksburg appear to be a mishmash of trees, Texas towns and former US presidents. But they were actually named so their initials spell out secret codes. The streets crossing Main St to the east of Courthouse Sq are Adams, Llano, Lincoln, Washington, Elk, Lee, Columbus, Olive, Mesquite and Eagle. And the streets to the west are Crockett, Orange, Milam, Edison, Bowie, Acorn, Cherry and Kay.

---

its share of touristy shops, Fredericksburg has retained the look (if not the feel) of 125 years ago.

Mid-May through June is peach-pickin' season around town. You can get them straight from the farm, and some farms will let you pick your own. Visit www.texaspeaches.com for a list of more than 20 local peach farms.

Thanks to its conducive terroir, the area is also becoming known for its prolific wineries. If winery-hopping is on the agenda, print a map from www.texaswinetrail.com or www.wineroad290.com.

**National Museum
of the Pacific War**   MUSEUM

(www.pacificwarmuseum.org; 340 E Main St; adult/child $14/7; ⊙9am-5pm) This museum complex consists of three war-centric galleries: the Admiral Nimitz Museum, chronicling the life and career of Fredericksburg's most famous son; the George HW Bush Gallery of the Pacific War, a large, impressive building housing big planes, big boats and big artillery; and the Pacific Combat Zone, a 3-acre site that's been transformed into a South Pacific battle zone.

**Enchanted Rock State
Natural Area**   PARK

(☑830-685-3636; www.tpwd.state.tx.us; 16710 RR 965; adult/child $7/free; ⊙8am-10pm) North of town about 18 miles, you'll find a dome of pink granite dating from the Proterozoic era rising 425ft above ground – one of the largest batholiths in the US. If you want to climb it, go early; gates close when the daily attendance quota is reached.

🛏 Sleeping & Eating

Fredericksburg is a popular weekend getaway, especially during the spring, when room rates are at their highest.

Gastehaus Schmidt   ACCOMMODATION SERVICES

(☑866-427-8374, 830-997-5612; www.fbglodging.com; 231 W Main St) Nearly 300 B&Bs do business in this county; this reservation service helps you sort them out.

Fredericksburg Inn & Suites   MOTEL $$

(☑830-997-0202; www.fredericksburg-inn.com; 201 S Washington St; d $110-180, ste $150-220; 🅿❄🛜🐾🐾) Tops in the midpriced-motel category, this place was built to look like the historic house it sits behind, and it succeeds. A fabulously inviting pool with a waterslide, a spacious hot tub and clean,

WALTER BIBIKOW / GETTY IMAGES ©

Main Street, Fredericksburg

updated rooms make it good value for the price.

Fredericksburg Herb Farm   COTTAGE $$$
(☑ 844-596-2302; www.fredericksburgherbfarm. com; 405 Whitney St; r from $180; P ✳ ☎) In a lushly landscaped setting on the west side of town, these comfy flower-trimmed cottages make for a peaceful getaway – particularly if you add in a spa treatment. The restaurant on-site serves excellent, seasonally inspired cuisine (mains $20 to $28); reserve well ahead.

Tubby's Ice House   CARIBBEAN $
(318 E Austin St; mains $6-10; ⊙ 11am-9pm Sun-Thu, to midnight Fri & Sat) One block from tourist-lined Main St, Tubby's draws a laid-back, mostly local crowd, who come for plates of pulled pork, jerk chicken, chili-glazed wings, cod fritters and other snacks, plus a fine selection of microbrews. The setting: colorful outdoor picnic tables; and there's a bocce court.

Pink Pig   AMERICAN $$
(☑ 830-990-8800; www.pinkpigtexas.com; 6266 E US Hwy 290; lunch $9-12, dinner $18-28; ⊙ 11am-2:30pm Tue & Wed, 11am-2:30pm & 5:30-9pm Thu-Sat, from 10am Sun) Pick up baked goods or a boxed lunch from the bakery counter, or enjoy a meal inside the historic log building. And save room for dessert: the Pink Pig was opened by Rebecca Rather, aka the Pastry Queen.

Hill Top Café   AMERICAN $$
(☑ 830-997-8922; 10661 N Hwy 87; mains lunch $9-18, dinner $19-30; ⊙ 11am-2pm & 5-9pm Tue-Sun) Located 10 miles north of town inside a renovated 1950s gas station, this cozy roadhouse serves up satisfying meals and Hill Country ambience at its best. Reservations recommended. On weekends it has live blues from the owner, Johnny Nicholas, a former member of the West Coast swing band Asleep at the Wheel. Reservations are recommended.

❶ Getting There & Away
You can get a shuttle service from the San Antonio airport through **Stagecoach Taxi and Shuttle** (☑ 830-385-7722; www.stagecoachtaxi andshuttle.com); the cost is $95 each way for up to four people. However, since driving around the Hill Country is half the fun, your best bet is to drive yourself.

Luckenbach
POP 3

As small as Luckenbach is – three permanent residents, not counting the cat – it's big on Texas charm.

The heart of the, er, action is the old trading post established back in 1849 – now the **Luckenbach General Store** (☑ 830-997-3224; www.luckenbachtexas.com; ⊙ 10am-9pm Mon-Sat, noon-9pm Sun).

Check www.luckenbachtexas.com for the music schedule. Sometimes the guitar picking starts at 1pm, sometimes 5pm, and weekends usually see live-music events in the old dance hall – a Texas classic. The 4th of July and Labor Day weekends are deluged with visitors going to the concerts.

We'd be remiss if we didn't mention that Luckenbach was made famous in a country song by Waylon Jennings – but we figured you either already knew that, or wouldn't really care.

From Fredericksburg, take US 290 east then take FM 1376 south for about 3 miles.

Johnson City & Stonewall

POP 1660

◉ Sights

Lyndon B Johnson Ranch HISTORIC SITE
See p26.

Johnson's Boyhood Home HISTORIC BUILDING
See p27.

🛏 Sleeping & Eating

There aren't many hotels or motels in the area, although a few B&Bs do solid business.

Chantilly Lace Country Inn B&B $$
(☑ 830-660-2621; www.chantillylacesoaps.com; 625 Nugent Ave, Johnson City; ste incl breakfast $125-149; ➔ ✳) The Chantilly Lace Country

---

WORTH A TRIP

GUADALUPE RIVER STATE PARK

Thirty miles north of San Antonio, this exceptionally beautiful park (☑ 830-438-2656; www.tpwd.state.tx.us; 3350 Park Rd 31, Spring Branch; adult/under 12yr $7/free, campsites $14-20; ⊙ dawn-dusk) straddles a 9-mile stretch of the sparklingly clear, bald-cypress-lined Guadalupe River, and it's great for canoeing and tubing. There are also 3 miles of hiking trails through the park's almost 2000 acres. Two-hour guided tours of the nearby Honey Creek State Natural Area are included in the price of admission. The tours leave at 9am on Saturday morning from the Guadalupe ranger station.

Inn in Johnson City offers Texas-style rooms that aren't as lacy and countrified as its name would imply.

Rose Hill Manor B&B $$$
(☑ 830-644-2247; www.rose-hill.com; 2614 Upper Albert Rd, Stonewall; ste incl breakfast $199-259; ➔ ✳ @) This exquisite B&B in Stonewall offers top-notch accommodation, with beautifully appointed suites and cottages.

Pecan Street Brewing PUB $
(☑ 830-868-2500; www.pecanstreetbrewing.com; 106 E Pecan Dr, Johnson City; mains $7-15; ⊙ 11am-9pm Tue-Thu, 8am-10pm Fri-Sun) A friendly neighborhood brewpub that serves up a variety of dishes alongside its own microbrews in a casual, friendly environment. It usually has live music on Saturday nights, which means it doubles as nightlife.

Austin

POP 912,800

You'll see it on bumper stickers and T-shirts throughout the city: 'Keep Austin Weird.' And while old-timers grumble that Austin has lost its funky charm, the city has still managed to hang on to its incredibly laid-back vibe. Though this former college town with a hippie soul has seen an influx of tech types and movie stars, it's still a town of artists with day jobs, where people try to focus on their music or write their novel or annoy their neighbors with crazy yard art.

Along the freeway and in the 'burbs, big-box stores and chain restaurants have proliferated at an alarming rate. But the neighborhoods still have an authentically Austin feel, with all sorts of interesting, locally owned businesses, including a flock of food trailers – a symbol of the low-key entrepreneurial spirit that represents Austin at its best.

The one thing everyone seems to know about Austin, whether they've been there or not, is that it's a music town, even if they don't actually use the words 'Live Music Capital of the World' (though that's a claim no one's disputing). The city now hosts two major music festivals, South by Southwest and the Austin City Limits festival, but you don't have to endure the crowds and exorbitant hotel prices to experience the scene, because Austin has live music all over town every night of the week.

Bob Bullock Texas State History Museum

◉ Sights

Don't limit yourself to the sights; Austin is about the experience. Bars, restaurants, even grocery stores and the airport have live music. And there are outdoor activities galore. A full day might also include shopping for some groovy vintage clothes, sipping a margarita at a patio cafe and lounging on the banks of Barton Springs. But if your vacation isn't complete without a visit to a museum, there are some stops that are worth your while.

Bob Bullock
Texas State History Museum   MUSEUM
(☑512-936-8746; www.thestoryoftexas.com; 1800 Congress Ave; adult/child $9/6; ☉9am-5pm Mon-Sat, noon-5pm Sun) This is no dusty old historical museum. Big, glitzy and still relatively new, it shows off the Lone Star State's history, all the way from when it used to be part of Mexico up to the present, with high-tech interactive exhibits and fun theatrics. Allow at least a few hours for your visit.

Blanton Museum of Art   MUSEUM
(☑512-471-5482; www.blantonmuseum.org; 200 E Martin Luther King Jr Blvd; adult/child $9/free; ☉10am-5pm Tue-Fri, 11am-5pm Sat, 1-5pm Sun) A big university with a big endowment is bound to have a big art collection, and now, finally, it has a suitable building in which to show it off properly. With one of the best university art collections in the USA, the Blanton showcases a variety of styles. It doesn't go in

much depth into any of them but then again you're bound to find something of interest.

Texas State Capitol   HISTORIC BUILDING
(☑512-463-5495, tours 512-463-0063; cnr 11th St & Congress Ave; ☉7am-10pm Mon-Fri, 9am-8pm Sat & Sun) FREE Built in 1888 from sunset-red granite, this state capitol is the largest in the US, backing up the ubiquitous claim that everything is bigger in Texas. If nothing else, take a peek at the lovely rotunda and try out the whispering gallery created by its curved ceiling.

Thinkery   MUSEUM
(☑512-469-6200; www.thinkeryaustin.org; 1830 Simond Ave; admission $9, child under 2yr free; ☉noon-5pm Mon, 10am-5pm Tue-Fri, to 6pm Sat & Sun; ⊞) This huge 40,000-sq-ft space north of downtown is an inspiring place for young minds, with hands-on activities in the realms of science, technology and the arts. Kids can get wet learning about fluid dynamics, build LED light structures and explore chemical reactions in the Kitchen Lab, among many other attractions. There's also an outdoor play area with nets and climbing toys.

🏃 Activities

Barton Springs Pool   SWIMMING
(☑512-867-3080; 2201 Barton Springs Rd; adult/child $4/2; ☉8am-10pm Fri-Wed late-Apr–Oct) Hot? Not for long. Even when the temperature hits 100, you'll be shivering in a jiff after you jump into this icy-cold natural-spring

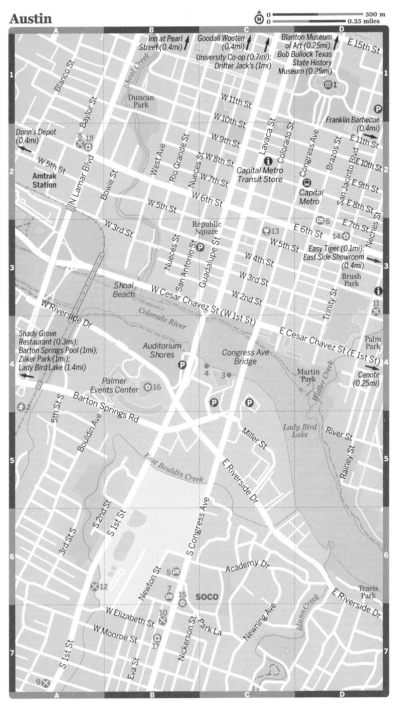

N 0 — 500 m
0 — 0.25 miles

Inn at Pearl Street (0.4mi)
Goodall Wooten (0.4mi)
University Co-op (0.7mi); Drifter Jack's (1mi)
Blanton Museum of Art (0.25mi); Bob Bullock Texas State History Museum (0.25mi)

E 15th St

Blanco St
Shoal Creek
Duncan Park
W 11th St
W 10th St
W 9th St
W 8th St
W 7th St
W 6th St
W 5th St

Baylor St
West Ave
Rio Grande St
Nueces St

Lavaca St
Colorado St
Congress Ave
Brazos St
San Jacinto Blvd
Neches St

E 11th St
E 10th St
E 9th St
E 8th St
E 7th St

Franklin Barbecue (0.4mi)

Donn's Depot (0.4mi)
W 5th St
Amtrak Station

N Lamar Blvd
Bowie St

Capital Metro Transit Store

Capital Metro

E 6th St
Republic Square
W 5th St
W 4th St
W 3rd St
W 2nd St

Nueces St
San Antonio St
Guadalupe St

Easy Tiger (0.1mi); East Side Showroom (0.4mi)

Brush Park

Shoal Beach
W Cesar Chavez St (W 1st St)
Colorado River

Trinity St

E Cesar Chavez St (E 1st St)

Palm Park

Shady Grove Restaurant (0.3mi); Barton Springs Pool (1mi); Zilker Park (1mi); Lady Bird Lake (1.4mi)

W Riverside Dr

Auditorium Shores
Congress Ave Bridge
Martin Park

Cenote (0.25mi)

Palmer Events Center
Barton Springs Rd

5th St
Bouldin Ave

Miller St
Lady Bird Lake
River St

East Bouldin Creek
E Riverside Dr

Waller Creek
Rainey St

S 2nd St
S 1st St
S Congress Ave

SOCO
Academy Dr

Travis Park

Newton St

E Riverside Dr

3rd St

W Elizabeth St
W Monroe St

Nickerson St
Park La
Newning Ave

Eva St

Bloom Creek

Austin

pool. Draped with century-old pecan trees, the area around the pool is a social scene in itself, and the place gets packed on hot summer days.

Lady Bird Lake CANOEING
(☑ 512-459-0999; www.rowingdock.com; 2418 Stratford Dr; ◷ 7:30am-8:30pm) Named after former first lady 'Lady Bird' Johnson, Lady Bird Lake kind of looks like a river. And no wonder: it's actually a dammed-off section of the Colorado River that divides Austin into north and south. Get out on the water at the Rowing Dock, which rents kayaks, canoes and stand-up paddleboards for $10 to $25 per hour.

Zilker Park PARK
(☑ 512-974-6700; www.austintexas.gov/department/zilker-metropolitan-park; 2100 Barton Springs Rd) This 350-acre park is a slice of green heaven, lined with hiking and biking trails. The park also provides access to the famed Barton Springs natural swimming pool and Barton Creek Greenbelt. Find boat rentals, a miniature train and a botanical garden, too. On weekends from April to early September, admission is $5 per car.

Bicycle Sport Shop BICYCLE RENTAL
(☑ 512-477-3472; www.bicyclesportshop.com; 517 S Lamar Blvd; per 2hr from $16; ◷ 10am-7pm Mon-Fri, 9am-6pm Sat, 11am-5pm Sun) The great thing about Bicycle Sport Shop is its proximity to Zilker Park, Barton Springs and the Lady Bird Lake bike paths, all of which are within a few blocks. Rentals range from $16 for a two-hour cruise on a standard bike, to $62 for a full day on a top-end full-suspension model. On weekends and holidays, advance reservations are advised.

★ Festivals & Events

Also check out the weekly *Austin Chronicle* (www.austinchronicle.com) for an events calendar.

South by Southwest MUSIC, FILM
(SXSW; www.sxsw.com; single festival $650-1300, combo pass $1025-1745) One of the American music industry's biggest gatherings has now expanded to include film and interactive media. Austin is absolutely besieged with visitors during this two-week window in mid-March, and many a new resident first came to the city to hear a little live music.

Austin City Limits Music Festival MUSIC
(www.aclfestival.com; 1-/3-day pass $100/250) What do music lovers do in autumn? The Austin City Limits festival, which is not as big as SXSW but has been swiftly gaining on it in terms of popularity. The three-day festival, held on eight stages in Zilker Park during October, books more than 100 pretty impressive acts and sells out months in advance.

Formula 1 Grand Prix SPORTS
(www.formula1.com; ◷ late Oct or Nov) In Travis County, just outside of Austin, a high-speed racetrack draws legions of F1 fans during a high-octane weekend in autumn.

☐ Sleeping

South Congress (SoCo) has the coolest and quirkiest digs, while downtown has more high-rent options. Check the Austin Visitor Information Center (p80).

Hotel rates soar and locals flee during SXSW and F1, so plan accordingly.

★ Firehouse Hostel
HOSTEL **$**

(☎512-201-2522; www.firehousehostel.com; 605 Brazos St; dm $32-40, r $110-170, ste $130-170; ☻❋@) A hostel in downtown Austin? Finally! And a pretty darned spiffy one, at that. Opened in January of 2013 in a former firehouse, it's still fresh and new, and the downtown location right across from the historic Driskill Hotel is as perfect as you can get.

Drifter Jack's
HOSTEL **$**

(☎512-243-8410; www.drifterjackshostel.com; 2602 Guadalupe St; dm $28-35, d $75-85; ❋@) Across from the University of Texas campus, Drifter Jack's is a friendly, laid-back place, with mural-covered rooms and a small lounge. The hostel draws mostly a young crowd (though all are welcome) and organizes pub crawls and otheroutings.

Goodall Wooten
HOSTEL **$**

(☎512-472-1343; 2112 Guadalupe St; r $35; ❋@) A private dorm near UT, 'the Woo' generally has rooms available mid-May to mid-August, and sometimes has space for travelers at other times of the year. Just the basics – expect sheets, toilet paper and a small refrigerator – but no decor. Cash only.

★ Hotel San José
BOUTIQUE HOTEL **$$**

(☎512-852-2360; www.sanjosehotel.com; 1316 S Congress Ave; r $215-360, r without bathroom $150, ste $335-500; P☻❋@) Local hotelier Liz Lambert revamped a 1930s-vintage motel into a chic SoCo retreat with minimalist rooms in stucco bungalows, a lovely bamboo-fringed pool, and a very Austin-esque hotel bar in the courtyard that's known for its celebrity-spotting potential. SoCo has become quite the scene, and this hotel's location puts you right in the thick of it.

★ Austin Motel
MOTEL **$$**

(☎512-441-1157; www.austinmotel.com; 1220 S Congress Ave; r $95-180, ste $207-225; P❋@) 'Garage-sale chic' is the unifying factor at this wonderfully funky motel that embodies the spirit of the 'Keep Austin Weird' movement. Each room is individually decorated with whatever happened to be lying around at the time, and with varying degrees of success. The excellent location, friendly staff and enticing pool make this a great choice.

Habitat Suites
HOTEL **$$**

(☎512-467-6000; www.habitatsuites.com; 500 E Highland Mall Blvd; ste $100-160; P☻❋@) ⌖ Locally owned and ecofriendly, this quiet place is tucked away just north of downtown, away from the hustle and bustle. The furnishings may be slightly past their prime, but practical travelers will get a lot for their money here.

Inn at Pearl Street
B&B **$$$**

(☎512-478-0051; www.innpearl.com; 809 W Martin Luther King Jr Blvd; d $195-245, ste $265-365; P☻❋@) This is a preservationist's dream come true. The owners picked up this run-down property, and completely restored it, decorating the whole place in a plush European style. The rooms come in a variety of flavors and are located in two separate buildings – Victoria House or Burton House – so check the website to find one that suits.

✗ Eating

It's easy to find good, affordable food in Austin. SoCo provides a slew of options, but you'll be competing with lots of other hungry diners for a table. Those in the know go instead to S 1st St (1400 to 2100 blocks), where Mexican herbalists and tattoo parlors alternate with trailer-park food courts and organic cafes. Barton Springs Rd (east of Lamar Blvd) also has a number of interesting eateries, and Guadalupe St, by UT, is the place to look for cheap eats. Some great meat-market barbecue is available in nearby central Texas.

Food truck, South Congress
KYLIE MCLAUGHLIN / GETTY IMAGES ©

MEALS ON WHEELS

Food trailers are here to stay – even if they can move around at whim. We haven't listed any of these rolling restaurants because of their transient nature, but instead invite you to explore some of the areas where they congregate. Wander from trailer to trailer till one strikes your fancy, or make a progressive dinner out of it. Look for clusters of Airstreams and taco trucks in some of these likely spots:

➡ **South Austin Trailer Park & Eatery** (1311 S 1st St) seems to be a rather settled trailer community, with a fence, an official name, a sign and picnic tables. Look for Torchy's Tacos, which whips up some of Austin's best tacos.

➡ **1503 S 1st St** has a cluster of food trailers, including Gourdough's, which serves gourmet doughnut combos, including a doughnut burger.

➡ **South Congress**, between Elizabeth and Monroe, yields lots of options, including the decadent Hey Cupcake!

➡ **East Austin** has its own little enclave, conveniently located right among all the bars on the corner of E 6th and Waller Sts. Five blocks further east you'll find East Side King, serving some of Austin's best (and spiciest!) Thai dishes (open nights only).

★ **Franklin Barbecue** BARBECUE $
(☑ 512-653-1187; www.franklinbarbecue.com; 900 E 11th St; mains $6-15; ⊙ 11am-2pm Tue-Sun) America's most famous barbecue spot only serves lunch, and only till it runs out – usually well before 2pm. In fact, to avoid missing out, you should join the line by 10am (9am on weekends). Just treat it as a tailgating party: bring beer or mimosas to share and make friends.

Stiles Switch BARBECUE $
(☑ 512-380-9199; 6610 N Lamar Blvd; mains $7-18; ⊙ 11am-9pm Tue-Sun) Stiles Switch has manageable lines: you won't have to suffer to enjoy outstanding brisket, fired up to tender, smoky perfection, at this popular eatery 6 miles north of downtown. Top it off with some ribs, a side of corn casserole and a local microbrew.

Cenote CAFE $
(1010 E Cesar Chavez St; mains $8-15; ⊙ 7am-11pm Mon-Fri, from 8am Sat, 8am-4pm Sun; 🖥) One of our favorite cafes in Austin, Cenote uses seasonal, largely organic ingredients in its simple but delicious anytime fare. Come for housemade granola and yogurt with fruit, banh mi sandwiches and couscous curry. The cleverly shaded patio is a fine retreat for a rich coffee or a craft beer (or perhaps a handmade popsicle from Juju).

Amy's Ice Cream ICE CREAM $
(☑ 512-480-0673; www.amysicecreams.com; 1012 W 6th St; ice cream $3-6; ⊙ 11:30am-midnight) It's not just the ice cream we love; it's the toppings that get pounded and blended in,

violently but lovingly, by the staff wielding a metal scoop in each hand. Look for other locations on Guadalupe St north of the UT campus, on South Congress near all the shops, or at the airport for a last-ditch fix.

Trudy's Texas Star TEX-MEX $
(☑ 512-477-2935; www.trudys.com; 409 W 30th St; mains $9-14; ⊙ 2pm-2am Mon-Thu, from 11am Fri, from 9am Sat & Sun) Get your Tex-Mex fix here; the menu is consistently good, with several healthier-than-usual options. But we'll let you in on a little secret: this place could serve nothing but beans and dirt and people would still line up for the margaritas, which might very well be the best in Austin.

Bouldin Creek Coffee House VEGETARIAN $
(☑ 512-416-1601; 1900 S 1st St; mains $6-10; ⊙ 7am-midnight Mon-Fri, 8am-midnight Sat & Sun; 🖥☑) You can get your veggie chorizo tacos or a potato leek omelet all day long at this buzzing vegan-vegetarian eatery. It's got an eclectic South Austin vibe and is a great place for people-watching, finishing your novel or joining a band.

Shady Grove Restaurant AMERICAN $
(☑ 512-474-9991; www.theshadygrove.com; 1624 Barton Springs Rd; mains $9-15; ⊙ 11am-10:30pm) The large patio with its tall shady pecan trees is a huge draw at this friendly, festive spot near Barton Springs. There's plenty of satisfying American and Tex-Mex dishes on hand, including chili cheese fries, a Hippie Sandwich (grilled veggies with mozzarella) and steak tacos.

★ **Güero's Taco Bar**   TEX-MEX **$$**

(☑512-447-7688; 1412 S Congress Ave; mains $6-15; ⊙11am-10pm) Set in a former feed-and-seed store from the late 1800s, Güero's is an Austin classic and always draws a crowd. Come for homemade corn tortillas (the tacos *al pastor* are excellent), chicken tortilla soup and refreshing margaritas. Head to the oak-shaded garden for live music (Wednesday through Sunday).

★ **Salt Lick Bar-B-Que**   BARBECUE **$$**

(☑512-858-4959; www.saltlickbbq.com; 18300 FM 1826, Driftwood; mains $10-17; ⊙11am-10pm; ⊕) It's worth the 20-mile drive out of town just to see the massive outdoor barbecue pits at this parklike place off US 290. It's a bit of a tourist fave, but the crowd-filled experience still gets our nod. BYOB. Hungry? Choose the family-style all-you-can-eat option (adult/child $25/9).

Laundrette   MODERN AMERICAN **$$**

(☑512-382-1599; 2115 Holly St; mains $18-24; ⊙5pm-10pm daily & 11am-2:30pm Sat & Sun) A brilliant repurposing of a former washateria, Laundrette boasts a stylish, streamlined design that provides a fine backdrop to the delicious Mediterranean-inspired cooking. Among the many hits: crab toast, wood-grilled octopus, brussels sprouts with apple-bacon marmalade, a perfectly rendered brick chicken and whole grilled branzino (European seabass).

Moonshine Patio Bar & Grill   AMERICAN **$$**

(☑512-236-9599; www.moonshinegrill.com; 303 Red River St; dinner mains $14-24; ⊙11am-10pm Mon-Thu, to 11pm Fri & Sat, 9am-2pm & 5-10pm Sun) Dating from the mid-1850s, this historic building is a remarkably well-preserved

---

GAY & LESBIAN AUSTIN

With a thriving gay population – not to mention pretty mellow straight people – Austin is arguably the most gay-friendly city in Texas. The Austin Gay & Lesbian Chamber of Commerce (www.aglcc.org) sponsors the Pride Parade in June, as well as smaller events throughout the year. The Austin Chronicle (www.austinchronicle.com) runs a gay event column among the weekly listings, and glossy magazine L Style/G Style (www.lstylegstyle.com) has a dual gal/guy focus.

---

homage to Austin's early days. Within its exposed limestone walls, you can enjoy upscale comfort food, half-price appetizers at happy hour or a lavish Sunday brunch buffet ($18). Or, chill on the patio under the shade of pecan trees.

Justine's   FRENCH **$$$**

(☑512-385-2900; www.justines1937.com; 4710 E 5th St; mains $20-28; ⊙6pm-1am Wed-Mon) With a lovely garden setting festooned with fairy lights, Justine's is a top spot for wowing a date. French onion soup, seared scallops and grilled pork chop are standouts on the small, classic brasserie menu. There are also a few more-creative changing daily specials such as pan-seared quail with parsnip casserole, or grilled swordfish with artichokes and cauliflower puree.

🍷 Drinking & Nightlife

There are bejillions of bars in Austin, so what follows is only a select few. The legendary 6th St bar scene spills onto nearby thoroughfares, especially Red River St.

Many places on 6th St (west of Red River St) are shot bars aimed at party-hardy college students and tourists, while the Red River establishments draw a more local crowd. The lounges around the Warehouse District (near the intersection of W 4th and Colorado Sts) are a bit more upscale. SoCo and East 6th (from Medina to Chicon Sts) cater to the more offbeat in eclectic Austin.

★ **East Side Showroom**   BAR

(☑512-467-4280; 1100 E 6th St; ⊙5pm-2am) With an ambience that would feel right at home in Brooklyn (in the late 1800s), this bar anchoring the lively east-side scene is full of hipsters soaking up the craft cocktails and bohemian atmosphere.

★ **Ginny's Little Longhorn Saloon**   BAR

(☑512-524-1291; 5434 Burnet Rd; ⊙5pm-midnight Tue & Wed, to 1am Thu-Sat, 2-10pm Sun) This funky little cinder-block building is one of those dive bars that Austinites love so very much – and did even before it became nationally famous for chickenshit bingo on Sunday night.

Easy Tiger   BEER GARDEN

(easytigeraustin.com; 709 E 6th St; ⊙11am-2am) A short stroll from the nightlife mayhem of 6th St, Easy Tiger feels like a secret hide-away, with a back patio overlooking

THE SWARM: AUSTIN'S BATS

Looking very much like a special effect from a B movie, a funnel cloud of up to 1.5 million Mexican free-tailed bats swarms from under the Congress Avenue Bridge nightly from late March to early November. Turns out, Austin isn't just the live-music capital of the world; it's also home to the largest urban bat population in North America.

Austinites have embraced the winged mammals – figuratively speaking of course – and gather to watch the bats' nightly exodus right around dusk as they leave for their evening meal. (Not to worry: the bats are looking for insects, and they mostly stay out of your hair.) There's lots of standing around parking lots and on the bridge itself, but if you want a more leisurely bat-watching experience, try the TGI Friday's restaurant by the Radisson Hotel on Lady Bird Lake, or the Lone Star Riverboat (☑ 512-327-1388; www.lonestarriverboat.com; adult/child $10/7) or Capital Cruises (☑ 512-480-9264; www.capitalcruises.com; adult/child $10/5) for bat-watching tours.

peaceful Waller Creek. You'll find good microbrews and snacks, plus an excellent bakery (open at 7am) in the entrance.

Garage   LOUNGE

(503 Colorado St; ⊙ 5pm-2am Mon-Sat) Hidden inside a parking garage, this cozy, dimly lit lounge draws a hip but not overly precious Austin crowd who give high marks to the first-rate cocktails, handsomely designed space and novel location.

☆ Entertainment

On any given Friday night there are several hundred acts playing in the town's 200 or so venues, and even on an off night (Monday and Tuesday are usually the slowest) you'll typically have your pick of more than two dozen performances.

To plan your attack, check out the free weekly *Austin Chronicle* or the Thursday edition of the *Austin American-Statesman*.

★ Continental Club   LIVE MUSIC

(☑ 512-441-2444; www.continentalclub.com; 1315 S Congress Ave; ⊙ 4pm-2am Tue-Sun, from 6pm Mon) No passive toe-tapping here; this 1950s-era lounge has a dancefloor that's always swinging with some of the city's best local acts.

Donn's Depot   LIVE MUSIC

(☑ 512-478-3142; donnsdepot.com; 1600 W 5th St; ⊙ 2pm-2am Mon-Fri, from 6pm Sat) Austin loves a dive bar, and Donn's combines a retro atmosphere inside an old railway car with live music six nights a week, including Donn himself performing alongside the Station Masters. A mix of young and old come to Donn's, and the dancefloor sees plenty of action.

Broken Spoke   LIVE MUSIC

(www.brokenspokeaustintx.com; 3201 S Lamar Blvd; ⊙ 11am-midnight Tue-Thu, to 1am Fri & Sat) With old wood floors and wagon-wheel chandeliers that George Strait once hung from, Broken Spoke is a true Texas honky-tonk.

Skylark Lounge   BLUES

(☑ 512-730-0759; www.skylarkaustin.com; 2039 Airport Blvd; ⊙ 5pm-midnight Mon-Sat, to 10pm Sun) It's a bit of a drive (2.5 miles northeast of downtown), but well worth the effort to reach this friendly dive bar that serves up live blues – along with fairly priced drinks, free popcorn and a shaded patio.

Long Center for the
Performing Arts   PERFORMING ARTS

(☑ 512-457-5100; www.thelongcenter.org; 701 W Riverside Dr) This state-of-the-art theater opened in late 2008 as part of a waterfront redevelopment along Lady Bird Lake. The multistage venue hosts drama, dance, concerts and comedy.

Alamo Drafthouse Cinema   CINEMA

(☑ 512-861-7020; www.drafthouse.com; 320 E 6th St; admission $11) Easily the most fun you can have at the movies: sing along with *Grease,* quote along with *Princess Bride,* or just enjoy food and drink delivered right to your seat during first-run films. Check the website for other locations.

TXRD Lonestar Rollergirls   SPECTATOR SPORT

(www.txrd.com) Get ready to rumble – it's roller-derby night and the Hellcat women skaters are expected to kick some Cherry Bomb ass. No matter who wins, the TXRD Lonestar Rollergirls league always puts on a good show, usually at the Palmer Events Center.

🛍 Shopping

Vintage is a lifestyle, and the city's best hunting grounds for retro fashions and furnishings are South Austin and Guadalupe St near UT. You can download a map at www.vintagearoundtownguide.com.

On the first Thursday of the month, S Congress Ave is definitely the place to be: stores stay open until 10pm and there's live entertainment.

★ Uncommon Objects   VINTAGE

(☎512-442-4000; 1512 S Congress Ave; ⊙11am-7pm Sun-Thu, to 8pm Fri & Sat) 'Curious oddities' are what they advertise at this quirky antique store that sells all manner of fabulous knickknacks, all displayed with an artful eye. More than 20 different vendors scour the state to stock their stalls, so there's plenty to look at.

Waterloo Records   MUSIC

(☎512-474-2500; www.waterloorecords.com; 600 N Lamar Blvd; ⊙10am-11pm Mon-Sat, from 11am Sun) If you want to stock up on music, this is the record store. There are sections reserved just for local bands, and listening stations featuring Texas, indie and alt-country acts.

University Co-op   SOUVENIRS

(☎512-476-7211; 2246 Guadalupe St; ⊙8:30am-7:30pm Mon-Fri, 9:30am-6pm Sat, 11am-5pm Sun) Stock up on souvenirs sporting the Longhorn logo at this store brimming with school spirit. It's amazing the sheer quantity of objects that come in burnt orange and white.

ℹ Information

Austin indoors is nonsmoking, period (even bars). A vast wi-fi network blankets downtown. City of Austin libraries have free internet.

Austin Visitor Information Center (☎512-478-0098; www.austintexas.org; 602 E 4th St; ⊙9am-5pm Mon-Sat, from 10am Sun) Helpful staff, free maps, extensive racks of information brochures and a sample of local souvenirs for sale.

FedEx Office (327 Congress Ave; ⊙7am-11pm Mon-Fri, 9am-9pm Sat & Sun) Internet access 30¢ a minute.

MEDIA

Austin American-Statesman (www.statesman.com) Daily newspaper.

Austin Chronicle (www.austinchronicle.com) Weekly newspaper, lots of entertainment info.

KLRU TV (www.klru.org) PBS affiliate with local programming that includes the popular music show *Austin City Limits*.

ℹ Getting There & Around

Austin-Bergstrom International Airport (AUS; www.austintexas.gov/airport) is off Hwy 71, southeast of downtown. The Airport Flyer (bus 100, $1.75) runs to downtown (7th St and Congress Ave) and UT (Congress Ave and 18th St) every 40 minutes or so. **SuperShuttle** (☎512-258-3826; www.supershuttle.com) charges around $16 from the airport to downtown. A taxi between the airport and downtown costs from $26 to $32. Most of the national rental-car companies are represented at the airport.

Aside from downtown and campus, parking is usually plentiful and free. Downtown meters (25c for 15 to 20 minutes) run late on weekends, including Sunday. The parking garage at 1201 San Jacinto is free for two hours and $2 per hour after that, maxing out at $8.

The downtown **Amtrak Station** (☎512-476-5684; www.amtrak.com; 250 N Lamar Blvd) is served by the *Texas Eagle*, which extends from Chicago to Los Angeles. The **Greyhound Bus Station** (☎512-458-4463; www.greyhound.com; 916 E Koenig Lane) is on the north side of town off I-35; take bus 7-Duval ($1.25) to downtown.

Austin's handy public transit system is run by **Capital Metro** (CapMetro; ☎512-474-1200; www.capmetro.org). Call for directions to anywhere or stop into the downtown **Capital Metro Transit Store** (209 W 9th St; ⊙7:30am-5:30pm Mon-Fri) for information.

Austinites are big bike fans. Join them by taking advantage of the shared biking scheme offered by **Austin B-cycle** (austin.bcycle.com), with self-checkout kiosks scattered around town.

Around Austin

Northwest of Austin along the Colorado River are the six Highland Lakes. One of the most popular lakes for recreation is the 19,000 sq acre Lake Travis off Hwy 71. Rent boats and Jet Skis at the associated marina, or overnight in the posh digs at Lakeway Resort and Spa (☎512-261-6600; www.lakewayresortandspa.com; 101 Lakeway Dr; r from $180; ⊛@🎧🗭). Lake Austin Spa Resort (☎512-372-7300; www.lakeaustin.com; 1705 S Quinlan Park Rd, off FM 2222; 3-night packages from $1850; ⊛@🗭) is the premier place to be pampered in the state. And Lake Travis has Texas' only official nude beach, Hippie Hollow (www.hippiehollow.com; 7000 Comanche Trail; day pass car/bicycle $15/8; ⊙9am-dusk Sep-May, 8am-dusk Jun-Aug). To get to Hippie Hollow from FM 2222, take Rte 620 south 1.5 miles to Comanche Trail and turn right. The entrance is 2 miles ahead on the left.

Wimberley

POP 2626

Even on weekends when there's no **market** (p29), there are plenty of shops to visit, stocked with antiques, gifts, and local arts and crafts. You can also taste olive oil in one of the state's only commercial olive orchards, eat expertly baked homemade pies or simply kick back at one of the many B&Bs along the creek.

For more information on market days and other happenings around town, contact the **Wimberley Convention & Visitors Bureau** (CVB; ☑ 512-847-2201; www.visitwimberley.com; 14001 RR 12; ☺ 9am-4pm Mon-Sat, noon-4pm Sun), near Brookshires grocery store.

⊙ Sights & Activities

Bella Vista Ranch   OLIVE ORCHARD
(☑ 512-847-6514; www.bvranch.com; 3101 Mt Sharp Rd, off CR 182; ☺ 10am-5pm Thu-Sat, noon-4pm Sun) An unusual sight in Wimberley (and the rest of Texas, for that matter) is the only producing olive orchard in the Hill Country, found at Bella Vista Ranch. It has a gift shop with free tastings as well as tours of the orchard and the olive press, one of only two in Texas.

Devil's Backbone   DRIVING
See p29.

Blue Hole   SWIMMING
See p29.

🛏 Sleeping & Eating

There are dozens of B&Bs and cottages in Wimberley; call the CVB or visit its website for more information.

Wimberley Inn   MOTEL $$
(☑ 512-847-3750; www.wimberleyinn.com; 200 RR 3237; d $89-149) Close to the action and just a quarter-mile east of the square, this motel has large rooms at a fair price. Standard rooms are inexpensive and simple, deluxe rooms step it up a notch. Either way, the grounds are lovely.

Blair House Inn   B&B $$
(☑ 512-847-1111, 877-549-5450; www.blairhouseinn.com; 100 Spoke Hill Rd; d $152-173, ste $220-240, cottages $275-300; 🐾🗑) Two miles south of town, this quiet, lovely B&B has eight rooms and two cabins. Some of the suites are knockouts, with big windows and stone fireplaces. There's also a cooking school, restau-

rant and spa on-site, so you can really hole up here for a while.

Leaning Pear   AMERICAN $
(☑ 512-847-7327; www.leaningpear.com; 111 River Rd; mains $7-9; ☺ 11am-3pm Sun, Mon, Wed & Thu, 11am-8pm Fri & Sat) Get out of the crowded downtown area for a relaxed lunch. This cafe exudes Hill Country charm like a cool glass of iced tea, with salads and sandwiches served in a restored stone house.

Wimberley Pie Company   DESSERTS $
(☑ 512-847-9462; www.wimberleypie.com; 13619 RR 12; ☺ 9:30am-5:30pm Tue-Fri, 10am-5pm Sat, noon-4pm Sun) You haven't eaten until you've wrapped your mouth around a pie from this small but popular bakery that supplies many of the area's restaurants (and a few in Austin) with every kind of pie and cheesecake you can imagine, and then some. It's about a quarter-mile east of the square.

Devil's Backbone Tavern
(☑ 830-964-2544; 4041 FM 32, Fischer; ☺ noon-midnight, to 1am Sat) About the only establishment on this stretch of road, Devil's Backbone Tavern is a perfectly tattered and dusty beer joint with a country-music jukebox and live acoustic music some nights.

🛍 Shopping

Art galleries, antique shops and craft stores surround Wimberley Square, located where Ranch Rd 12 crosses Cypress Creek and bends into an 'S.' The best browsing is 1½ miles north of the square on Ranch Rd 12 at **Poco Rio** (15406 RR 12), a shopping center with boutique clothing stores, artists' galleries, eateries, a health spa for acupuncture and massage, and an 18-hole putt-putt golf course, all set among lush gardens and tree-shaded pathways.

❶ Getting There & Away

To make the 1½-hour drive from Austin, take US 290 west to Dripping Springs, then turn left onto Ranch Rd 12. From San Antonio, take I-35 north to San Marcos, where you can pick up Ranch Rd 12 headed west and then north into town.

San Marcos

As well as being synonymous with outlet malls, San Marcos is home to Texas State University, and to both natural and tourist-built attractions.

⊙ Sights & Activities

Wittliff Collections
ARTS CENTER

(☎ 512-245-2313; www.thewittliffcollections.tx
state.edu; Alkek Library, TSU; ⊙ 8am-5pm Mon-Fri,
from 11am Sat, 2-6pm Sun) **FREE** Screenwriter/
photographer Bill Wittliff founded this
repository of literary and photographic
archives on the campus of Texas State University. Check out the excellent (and free!)
photographic exhibits. The 6600 sq ft of gallery space is room enough for several exhibitions, which always includes the Lonesome
Dove Collection.

The Wittliff Collections is located on the
7th floor of the Alkek Library. Look online
for directions on how to get there.

Aquarena Center
OUTDOORS

(Aquarena Springs; ☎ 512-245-7570; www.aqua
rena.txstate.edu; 167 Spring Lake; tours adult/child
4-15yr $9/6; ⊙ 10am-5pm, later in summer) **FREE**
Famed for its glass-bottom boat tours, this
enjoyable place is home to family-oriented
exhibitions on ecology, history and archae-
ology. It also includes the ruins of a Spanish
mission founded here on the Feast of San
Marcos.

Boat tours last an hour and let visitors
peep beneath the surface of the lake formed
by the town's namesake springs, which gush
forth 1½ million gallons of artesian water
every day.

San Marcos Lions Club Tube Rental
RIVER TUBING

(☎ 512-396-5466; www.tubesanmarcos.com; tubes
$8-10; ⊙ 10am-7pm daily Jun-Aug, Sat & Sun May &
Sep) Just south of the Aquarena Center, the
Lions Club rents tubes in City Park (next to
the Texas National Guard Armory) to tackle
a usually docile stretch of the San Marcos
River. The last tube is rented at 5:30pm and
the last shuttle pickup from Rio Vista Dam
is at 6:45pm sharp.

Wonder World
CAVE

(☎ 512-392-3760; www.wonderworldpark.com;
1000 Prospect St; combination tickets adult/
child 3-5yr $20/8.50; ⊙ 8am-8pm daily Jun-Aug,
9am-5pm Mon-Fri & to 6pm Sat & Sun Sep-May) A
mini-theme park has been built around this
earthquake-created cave – the most visited
cave in Texas. Take a one-hour tour through
the Balcones Fault Line Cave, where you can
look at the Edwards Aquifer up close; tours
leave every 15 to 30 minutes year-round.
Outside, in the 110ft Tejas Observation
Tower, you can make out the fault line itself.

Other attractions include a petting park
filled with Texas animals, a train ride around
the park and the quaint 'Anti-Gravity House,'
a holdover from family vacations of yester-
year. There's a picnic area on the grounds.

🛏 Sleeping & Eating

Chains abound 'round these parts, both for
sleeping and eating, especially along I-35.
However, since San Marcos is so close to San

Gruene Hall (p30)

Antonio, visitors rarely need to avail themselves of overnight accommodations.

Viola Street Inn B&B $$
([☑]512-392-6242; www.violastreetinn.com; 714 Viola St; d $95-160; [P][⊖][❋][🛜]) Awash in antiques, floral prints and Victorian charm, this inn takes traditional bed-and-breakfast style to the max. Relax in one of several lavish common areas or sit a spell on the sprawling front porch. Two of the four rooms have big ol' Jacuzzi tubs in the over-size bathrooms.

Railyard Bar & Grill AMERICAN $
([☑]512-392-7555; www.railyardbarandgrill.com; 116 S Edward Gary St; dishes $4-8; [⊙]11am-2am Tue-Sat, to midnight Sun & Mon) Grab some fried pickles and play a game of ping pong, or enjoy a burger and beer while watching a game of horseshoes out on the patio. No surprise that the Railyard is a popular hangout for college students; the vibe is easy and casual and there's plenty to keep you entertained.

Root Cellar Cafe CAFE $$
([☑]512-392-5158; www.rootcellarcafe.com; 215 N LBJ Dr; mains breakfast & lunch $4-10, dinner $9-25; [⊙]7am-10pm Tue-Sun) This intimate little cafe sits a few steps below street level and has rock walls, but that's where the similarity to an actual root cellar ends. The atmosphere is on the cozy side of upscale, with local art adorning the walls of the small dining rooms. Lots of tempting menu choices make it a no-brainer when you're looking for a more grown-up lunch or dinner.

 Drinking & Nightlife

Cheatham St Warehouse LIVE MUSIC
([☑]512-353-7777; www.cheathamstreet.com; 119 Cheatham St; [⊙]3pm-2am Mon-Fri, from 4pm Sat, 4-8pm Sun) Down by the railroad tracks in an old warehouse covered in corrugated tin sits this 1970s-era honky-tonk that has helped launch many a career, including George Strait's and Stevie Ray Vaughan's, both of whom had regular gigs here in the early days. Its signature event is the Wednesday night Songwriters Circle. You can catch free shows during happy hour every weekday between 5:30pm and 7pm.

 Shopping

San Marcos Premium Outlets MALL
([☑]512-396-2200; www.premiumoutlets.com; 3939 S IH-35, exit 200; [⊙]10am-9pm Mon-Sat, to 7pm

Sun) Outlet shops at this enormous mall offer at least a 30% discount on regular retail prices, and sometimes as much as 75% off. Stores include Last Call by Neiman Marcus, Tory Burch, Calvin Klein, J.Crew and Coach, just to name a few.

Tanger Outlets MALL
([☑]512-396-7446; www.tangeroutlet.com/sanmarcos; 4015 S IH-35; [⊙]9am-9pm Mon-Sat, 10am-7pm Sun) What? You're not exhausted yet? You still have money left to spend? Just south of Premium Outlets is the Tanger Outlet center – if you weren't paying attention, you might not even notice it's a separate mall.

Stores include a few big names, but for the most part they're not as high end as they are across the street. Think Old Navy, Van Heusen, Reebok and such.

ⓘ Information

The **San Marcos Tourist Information Center** ([☑]512-393-5930; www.toursanmarcos.com; 617 N IH-35, exit 204B/205; [⊙]9am-5pm Mon-Sat, 10am-4pm Sun) has maps, brochures and information on trolley tours of the town's historic districts.

Gruene

False-front wood buildings and old German homes make this the quintessential rustic Texas town. All of Gruene (pronounced 'green') is on the National Historic Register – and boy, do day-trippers know it. You won't be alone wandering among the antique, arts-and-crafts and knickknack shops.

◉ Sights & Activities

Gruene Hall DANCE HALL
See p30.

Rockin' R River Rides WATER SPORTS
([☑]830-629-9999; www.rockinr.com; 1405 Gruene Rd; tubes $20) This popular outfit offers inner tube rides for a scenic float along the Guadalupe River.

🛏 Sleeping & Eating

Gruene Mansion Inn INN $$$
([☑]830-629-2641; www.gruenemansioninn.com; 1275 Gruene Rd; d $190-260) This cluster of buildings is practically its own village, with rooms in the mansion, a former carriage house and the old barns. Richly decorated in a style the owners call 'rustic Victorian

elegance,' the rooms feature lots of wood, floral prints and pressed-tin ceiling tiles. Two-night minimum.

Gristmill Restaurant AMERICAN **$$**
(www.gristmillrestaurant.com; 1287 Gruene Rd; mains $10-24; ⊙11am-9pm Sun-Thu, to 10pm Fri & Sat) Behind Gruene Hall and right under the water tower, this restaurant is located within the brick remnants of a long-gone gristmill. Indoor seating affords a rustic ambience, while outdoor tables get a view of the river.

ⓘ Getting There & Away

Gruene is just off I-10 and Rte 46, 45 miles south of Austin and 25 miles northeast of San Antonio.

New Braunfels

The richly historic town of New Braunfels (named for its Prussian founder, Prince Carl of Solms Braunfels) was the first German settlement in Texas. Today residents from Austin and San Antonio flock to New Braunfels in summer for its main attraction: the cool and easy-flowing waters of the Guadalupe and Comal Rivers.

⊙ Sights & Activities

Floating down the Guadalupe in an inner tube is a Texas summer tradition. For the most part, the river is calm, with a few good rapids to make things exciting.

Dozens of local outfitters rent tubes, rafts, kayaks and canoes, then bus you upstream so you can float the three to four hours back to base. Put a plastic cooler full of snacks and beverages (no bottles) in a bottom-fortified tube next to you and make a day of it. Don't forget to bring sunscreen, a hat and drinking water. Wear shoes or sandals that you don't mind getting wet.

The bottom-fortified tubes cost $2 more than a regular old inner tube, but it's worth the splurge to keep your backside from scraping on the rocks that line the riverbed. Most outfitters offer coupons on their websites that will help defray the cost so you can treat yourself to a luxury ride. The waterway gets rockier the longer the region goes without rain, which can be for months during summer. The outfitters listed here all have current river conditions listed on their website so you'll know what to expect.

You can rent tubes from Gruene River Company (⊘830-625-2800; www.grueneriver company.com; 1404 Gruene Rd; tubes $17), Riverbank Outfitters (⊘830-625-4928; www.river bankoutfitters.com; 6000 River Rd; tubes $17) and Rockin' R River Rides (p30).

McKenna Children's Museum MUSEUM
(⊘830-606-9525; www.mckennakids.org; 801 W San Antonio St; late May–early Sep $7.50, early Sep–late May $5.50; ⊙10am-5pm Mon-Sat) Looking for family fun on dry land? Kids can explore everything from outer space to dude ranches at the McKenna Children's Museum. The Shadow Room is particularly mesmerizing, with interactive graphics that respond to kids' movements.

Schlitterbahn Waterpark Resort SWIMMING
(⊘830-625-2351; www.schlitterbahn.com; 400 Liberty Ave; all-day pass adult/child $48/38; ⊙10am-6pm or later daily late May-early Sep, Sat & Sun early May & late Sep) For an exhilarating experience, try Texas' largest water park, featuring about 30 different slides and water pools all using water from the Comal River. It's one of the best places to be with kids on a hot day.

Landa Park PARK
(⊘830-221-4350; 110 Golf Course Dr; park admission free) If you don't have a full day but still want to splash around a little, head to this scenic community park just west of Schlitterbahn. The park has an Olympic-size swimming pool (350 Aquatic Circle, summer only, adult/child $4/3), an 18-hole golf course ($2), a miniature railroad ($2.50), paddleboats ($3) and shady picnic facilities. All have different opening hours, so call first.

City Tube Chute WATER SPORTS
(⊘830-608-2165; 100 Leibscher Dr; admission $5, tube rental $7; ⊙10am-7pm daily Jun-Aug, Sat & Sun May) In Price Solms Park, the City Tube Chute is like a water slide for your inner tube that shoots you around a dam on the Comal River. Parking costs $5 on weekends.

⚏ Sleeping & Eating

Faust Hotel HISTORIC HOTEL **$$**
(⊘830-625-7791; www.fausthotel.com; 240 S Seguin Ave; d $79-149, ste $169-189) Built in the 1920s as a travelers' hotel, the Faust retains its old-fashioned charm – while the rooms have been updated, there's still plenty of evidence of the hotel's historic roots. The cheapest rooms are rather small, but they're a great deal, all things considered.

LULING

Luling trumpets that it's the 'crossroads to everywhere.' But the main reason to stop here these days as you whiz through on the way to Shiner is to see the annual Luling Watermelon Thump, which has been covered in *People* magazine and the *New York Times*. The famous fruit-growing contest, complete with a crowned queen, takes place the last full weekend of June. (Incidentally, Luling is also the two-time holder of the world watermelon-seed-spitting championship, as documented in the *Guinness Book of World Records*.)

Luling was founded as the western end of the Sunset branch of the Southern Pacific Railroad in 1874, and in 1922 oil was discovered beneath it. The downtown Central Texas Oil Patch Museum (☑830-875-1922; www.lulingoilmuseum.org; 421 E Davis St; admission by donation; ☺9am-4pm Mon-Fri, 10am-2pm Sat) is dedicated to Luling's history and heritage. In the same building, the Luling Chamber of Commerce (☑830-875-3214; www.lulingcc.org) has more information on the area, including its antiques shops.

Luling is on US 183 where it meets Hwys 80 and 90, just north of I-10; it's about an hour's drive from San Antonio or Austin, and is served by Greyhound.

Prince Solms' Inn   B&B $$

(☑800-625-9169, 830-625-9169; www.princesolmsinn.com; 295 E San Antonio St; d $125, ste $150) With a convenient downtown location, the popular Prince Solms' Inn is one of the oldest still-operating inns in Texas. Its floral Victorian and rustic Western-themed rooms offer authentic furnishings, and there is a variety of accommodations for groups of up to six people ($175 to $195). The romantic cabin out back has a full kitchen.

Naegelin's Bakery   BAKERY $

(☑830-625-5722; www.naegelins.com; 129 S Seguin Ave; ☺6:30am-5:30pm Mon-Fri, to 5pm Sat) More than just a great place to pick up German strudels and Czech kolaches, Naegelin's is also the oldest bakery in Texas; having opened in 1868, it's got nearly 150 years under its belt.

Faust Brewing Co   PUB $$

(☑830-625-7791; www.faustbrewing.com; 240 S Seguin Ave; mains $8-14; ☺4pm-midnight Mon-Thu, noon-midnight Fri-Sun) Located in the Faust Hotel, this convivial pub complements its microbrews with bar food with a German twist – perfectly befitting its setting in this oh-so-German town. It's known for its German nachos: housemade potato chips topped with brats, sauerkraut and beer cheese sauce.

Huisache Grill & Wine Bar   AMERICAN $$

(☑830-620-9001; www.huisache.com; 303 W San Antonio St; mains $9-19; ☺11am-10pm) Located in a converted home, this cozy, stylish eatery breaks with local tradition by not being even remotely German. An impressively lengthy wine list is one of the draws, as is the variety of the men, with everything from sandwiches to seafood and steaks.

Friesenhaus   GERMAN $$

(☑830-625-1040; www.friesenhausnb.com; 148 South Castell Ave; lunch $9, dinner mains $11-18; ☺11am-10pm Mon-Sat, to 9pm Sun; 🖟🐾) Schnitzel, *leberkäse* and *sauerbraten* are among the specialties you can expect at this German restaurant and bakery. (It also serves several fish dishes if you're not into meat.) On Friday and Saturday nights, you can enjoy your meal to the tune of German accordion music, and dogs are welcome in the lively *biergarten*.

Myron's Prime Steakhouse   STEAKHOUSE $$$

(☑830-624-1024; www.myronsprime.com; 136 N Castell Ave; mains $23-43; ☺4-10pm Mon-Thu, to 11pm Fri & Sat) Despite its location in the old Palace Movie Theatre, Myron's isn't the place to go for kitsch. The atmosphere – and the steaks – are serious.

ℹ️ Information

Visit the Greater New Braunfels **Chamber of Commerce** (☑800-572-2626; www.nbcham.org; 390 S Seguin Ave; ☺8am-5pm Mon-Fri) or the highway **visitors center** (☑830-625-7973; 237 IH-35 N; ☺9am-5pm) to pick up maps, historic downtown walking-tour brochures and loads more information on local attractions.

STRETCH YOUR LEGS
SAN ANTONIO

Start/Finish: The Alamo

Distance: 2.2 miles/3.5km

Duration: Three hours

Sprawling San Antonio has lots to offer, but it packs its best attractions into a relatively small area – perfect for exploring on foot. Head downtown to hit the highlights, including the Alamo and the Riverwalk.

Take this walk on Trip

1

The Alamo

Snap an iconic picture of the most cherished monument in all of Texas. If you have time, go inside and learn how the former mission became a famous military fort (☏210-225-1391; www.thealamo.org; 300 Alamo Plaza; ⊙9am-5:30pm Mon-Sat, from 10am Sun). For many, it's not so much a tourist attraction as a pilgrimage, and you might see visitors getting downright dewy-eyed at the description of how a few hundred revolutionaries died defending the fort against thousands of Mexican troops.

The Walk » Go west two blocks on Houston St.

Buckhorn Saloon & Museum

Enjoy a beverage amidst an impressive number of mounted animals, including a giraffe, a bear and all manner of horn-wielding mammals. If that doesn't quench your thirst for taxidermy, pony up for a kitsch adventure at the Buckhorn Museum (☏210-247-4000; www.buckhornmuseum.com; 318 E Houston St; adult/child 3-11yr $19/15; ⊙10am-5pm, to 8pm summer) that includes wildlife from all over the world, as well as oddities like a two-headed cow and eight-legged lamb.

The Walk » Turn right on Presa St. Right before the bridge, you'll find a set of stairs leading down to the Riverwalk. At the bottom, turn right.

Riverwalk

Another of San Antonio's star attractions, the Riverwalk is a charming European-style canal that sits below street level. It gets mighty crowded, but it takes you past colorful cafes, landscaped hotel gardens and stone footbridges that stretch over the water. For the best overview, hop on a 40-minute Rio San Antonio Cruise (☏800-417-4139; www.riosanantonio.com; adult/child under 5yr $8.25/2; ⊙9am-9pm).

The Walk » Past St Marys St, turn left then take the Drury footbridge over the water. Ascend to Market St, then turn right. Take a moment to notice the imposing red-granite Bexar County Courthouse on the left.

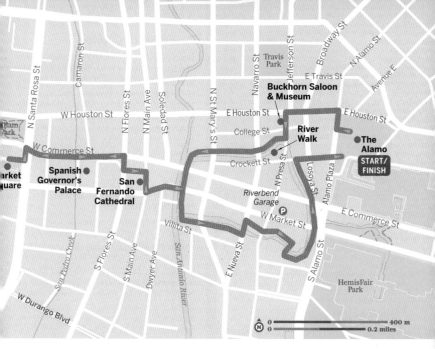

San Fernando Cathedral

San Fernando Cathedral (www.sfcathe dral.org; 115 Main Plaza; donations welcome; ⊘9am-5pm Tue-Fri, to 6:30pm Sat, 8:30-5pm Sun) became an important landmark when Mexican General Santa Ana took it over during the Battle of the Alamo. A hundred years later, some remains were uncovered that were purported to be those of Davy Crockett, William Travis and James Bowie. Pay your respects to whoever they are at the marble casket near the left entrance, and don't miss the dazzling gilt retablo behind the main altar.

The Walk » Take the path to the right of the cathedral. Cross Military Plaza, then walk around the stately City Hall, built in 1892.

Spanish Governor's Palace

A National Historic Landmark, this low-profile adobe building from the 1700s was neither a palace nor the home of the Spanish governor, but the residence of the presidio captain and seat of Texas' coloni- al government. During the 20th century, it held businesses including a saloon and a

pawn shop, but the city finally realized its significance, bought it back, and restored it to its former state.

The Walk » Take Commerce St two blocks west. A sidewalk from Santa Rosa St leads into the square.

Market Square

Mexican food, mariachi bands and a Mexican-style market await at Market Sq, which is a fair approximation of a trip south of the border. Wander the booths of the *mercado* and stock up on paper flowers, colorful pottery and the Virgin Mary in every conceivable medium. Grab some Mexican food and margaritas at the sprawling Mi Tierra (☐210-225-1262; www.mitierracafe.com; 218 Produce Row; mains $12-16; ⊘24hr).

The Walk » Return to the Riverwalk. After the Drury footbridge, go right then turn left to continue your route on the serene southern stretch. Emerge at Crockett St and turn right to return to the start.

STRETCH
YOUR LEGS
AUSTIN

Start/Finish: Texas State Capitol

Distance: 4.1 miles/6.6km

Duration: Four to five hours

Get to the heart of this immensely popular city on this downtown walking tour. You'll get a peek at many of the things that have indelibly shaped Austin's character – everything from Texas politics to campus life to Mexican free-tailed bats.

Take this walk on Trip

Texas State Capitol

Built in 1888 from sunset-red granite, the Texas State Capitol is the largest in the US. Pick up a brochure outlining a self-guided tour of the capitol building and grounds inside the tour-guide office on the ground floor. If nothing else, take a peek at the lovely rotunda and try out the whispering gallery created by its curved ceiling.

The Walk » Head up Congress Ave towards the University; it's just a few short blocks.

Bob Bullock Texas State History Museum

Big, glitzy and still relatively new, the Bullock (512-936-8746; www.thestoryof texas.com; 1800 Congress Ave; adult/child 4-17yr $9/6, Texas Spirit film $5/4; ☺9am-6pm Mon-Sat, noon-6pm Sun) shows off the Lone Star State's history, from when it used to be part of Mexico up to the present, with high-tech interactive exhibits and fun theatrics. The museum's most famous resident is the grotesquely proportioned Goddess of Liberty that stood atop the capitol for nearly 100 years. Allow at least an hour or two if you stop in.

The Walk » Go west one block up MLK Blvd, then turn right on University Ave and walk the two blocks to 21st St, where you'll find a postcard-perfect view of the University of Texas.

University of Texas

You could wander UT all day and still not see all of it, but this is probably the prettiest spot on campus and definitely the most iconic. Littlefield Fountain features a dramatic, European-style sculpture, and behind it stretches the gently sloping South Mall, a grassy lawn flanked by 80-year-old oak trees. Topping it off is the Main Building, whose tower is one of the most recognizable symbols of UT and Austin.

The Walk » Stroll up the South Mall to the Main Building, then turn left and cross the West Mall to get to Guadalupe St.

The Drag

Running along the west side of campus, Guadalupe St – aka 'The Drag' – is a bustling corridor lined with restaurants and shops. Join the pedestrians streaming up and down the west side of the street and grab a snack at one of the cheap eateries located along this stretch. Stock up on Longhorn souvenirs at the University Co-op (☑512-476-7211; 2246 Guadalupe St; ⊙8:30am-7:30pm Mon-Fri, 9:30am-6pm Sat, 11am-5pm Sun), selling a huge quantity of objects in burnt orange and white.

The Walk » Walk down Guadalupe St to MLK, then jog over one block to Lavaca. At the corner of 11th and Lavaca Sts, notice the Texas Governor's Mansion (and try not to get jumped by Secret Service). Continue south and turn right on 7th St.

Bremond Block

Part of the National Register of Historic Places, the Bremond Block preserves a concentration of elegant Victorian mansions with sprawling lawns and mature live oak trees. On the corner of Guadalupe, the 1886 John Bremond House is the most impressive example. Take the right fork of 7th St and circle the block clockwise to see them all.

The Walk » Walk east to Congress Ave and head south to the Colorado River.

Congress Ave Bridge

If you can time your last stop right – dusk, between late March and early November – you'll see the world's largest urban bat colony making their nightly exodus from under the bridge.

The Walk » Stroll back up Congress Ave (which is well lit, well populated and completely safe at night) to return to the starting point. Sixth St east of Congress is lined with bars, making it party central come nightfall.

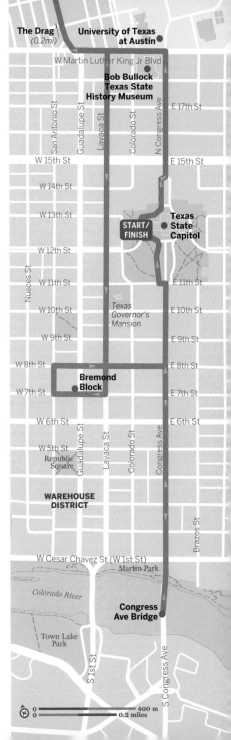

Big Bend & West Texas

The small towns of west Texas have become more than just the gateway to Big Bend National Park. Fort Davis, Marfa, Alpine and Marathon have a sprawling, easygoing charm and plenty of ways to keep a road-tripper entertained.

Welcome to the land of wide open spaces. Along I-10 there's not much to look at – just scrub brush and lots of sky – but dip beyond the interstate and you'll find vistas that are as captivating as they are endless. Sometimes the rugged terrain looks like the backdrop in an old Western movie; other times it looks like an alien landscape, with huge rock formations suddenly jutting out of the desert.

But what is there to do? Plenty. Exploring an enormous national park that's nearly the size of Rhode Island. Stopping in small towns that surprise you with minimalist art, planet-watching parties or fascinating ghost-town ruins. Chatting with friendly locals whenever the mood strikes you. And letting the slowness of west Texas get thoroughly under your skin.

ℹ WHAT TIME IS IT?

When it comes to time zones, El Paso sides with New Mexico, conforming to Mountain Time rather than Central Time like the rest of Texas. Confusing? Occasionally. If you're telling someone in neighboring Van Horn or Fort Stockton what time you'll meet them, be sure to add on the extra hour you'll lose just by leaving El Paso.

El Paso

Well, you've made it. You're just about as far west in Texas as you can go. Surrounded mostly by New Mexico and Mexico, El Paso seems to have more in common with its non-Texas neighbors than it does with Texas itself.

Sadly, El Paso and its sister city – Ciudad Juárez, Mexico, which is right across the river – have had a bit of a falling out. At one time, the two cities were inextricably linked, with tourists streaming back and forth across the Good Neighbor International Bridge all day long. But with the rise in gang- and drug-related violence, Juárez has become so dangerous that there is now little traffic between the two sides.

◎ Sights & Activities

★ **El Paso Museum of Art**   MUSEUM
See p34.

El Paso Holocaust Museum   MUSEUM
See p34.

Franklin Mountains State Park   PARK
(www.tpwd.state.tx.us; Transmountain Rd; adult/child $5/free; ⊗8am-5pm Mon-Fri, 6:30am-8pm Sat & Sun) At over 24,000 acres, this is the largest urban park in the US. It's a quick escape from the city to the home of ringtail cats, coyotes and countless other

smaller animals and reptiles. There's excellent mountain biking and hiking here, with 7192ft North Franklin Peak looming overhead.

Wyler Aerial Tramway CABLE CAR
(☎915-566-6622; 1700 McKinley Ave; adult/child under 12yr $8/4; ⊙noon-7pm Fri & Sat, 10am-5pm Sun) Sure, you'd feel a sense of accomplishment if you hiked to the top of the Franklin Mountains. We're not suggesting you take the easy way out (or are we?), but it only takes about four minutes to take a gondola to the top. After gliding 2600ft and gaining 940ft in elevation, you'll reach the viewing platform on top of Ranger Peak, where you'll enjoy spectacular views of Texas, New Mexico and Mexico.

🛏 Sleeping

In addition to the following exceptions, there are scads of characterless chain motels found along I-10.

Gardner Hotel HOSTEL $
(☎915-532-3661; www.gardnerhotel.com; 311 E Franklin Ave; r $60-70; 🛜) El Paso's oldest continually operating hotel is also the only real downtown bargain. It probably hasn't changed a whole lot since John Dillinger stayed here in the 1930s (hint: room 221 is where the outlaw slept), but it has a certain ragtag charm.

Coral Motel MOTEL $
(☎915-772-3263; www.coralmotel.net; 6420 Montana Ave; r $45-60; 🅿✻🛜) Anyone who loves 1950s roadside nostalgia will feel right at home at this friendly little motel with its Spanish-style barrel-tile roof and Jetsons-esque sign. Rooms are simple with white cinder-block walls, floral bedspreads and dated bathrooms, but you can't beat the price.

Camino Real Hotel HOTEL $$
(☎915-534-3000; www.caminorealelpaso.com; 101 S El Paso St; r weekday/weekend from $92/81; 🅿✻@🛜♨) The only US location of an upscale Mexican hotel chain, the historic Camino Real – in operation for over 100 years – has a prime location steps from downtown museums; a gorgeous bar with a Tiffany art glass dome; large, comfortable rooms; and friendly service, even when it's packed with conventioneers.

ⓘ HOT TOPIC: MEXICO BORDERLANDS
Tex has always mixed well with Mex. But the flow of Texans casually crossing from El Paso into Mexican border towns has slowed to a trickle due to drug-cartel-related violence. The state department urges caution when visiting all border towns in Mexico – as do we.

🍴 Eating

Mexican is the food of choice in El Paso; the town's known for a special bright-red chili-and-tomato sauce used on enchiladas. Tex-Mex in El Paso is cheap and abundant.

Craft & Social AMERICAN $
(www.craftandsocial.com; 305 E Franklin St; mains $7-11; ⊙11am-11pm Mon-Wed, to 2am Thu & Fri, 3pm-2am Sat, 4pm-midnight Sun) A welcome addition to El Paso, Craft & Social whips up high-end sandwiches (featuring ingredients such as oven-roasted chicken, brie and roasted red peppers), artisanal cheese and smoked-meat platters, and zesty salads. All go nicely with the craft brews from Belgium, Germany and the USA.

It's an appealing, anytime sort of place, with bar stools, communal tables, a few armchairs and sidewalk seating.

L&J Cafe MEXICAN $
(☎915-566-8418; http://landjcafe.com; 3622 E Missouri Ave; mains $5-13; ⊙9am-9pm) One of El Paso's best-loved Mexican joints, L&J serves up delicious tacos, fajitas and famous green-chile chicken enchiladas – plus a legendary menudo on weekends. It's next to the historic Concordia Cemetery, and at first glance looks a bit divey. Don't be deterred: it's been open since 1927, and the inside is much more inviting than the outside.

★ Tabla TAPAS $$
(115 Durango St; small plates $7-16; ⊙11am-10pm Mon-Thu, to 11pm Fri & Sat) Get ready to share all sorts of awesomeness. The small plates here fuse Spanish classics with the flavors of the Southwest in mouthwatering combos like short rib and blue-cheese croquettes, grilled octopus with *chimichurri*, and pork confit sliders. Tabla is set in a beautifully converted brick warehouse with tall ceilings and an open kitchen.

Guadalupe Mountains National Park

TIM FITZHARRIS / GETTY IMAGES ©

Crave   AMERICAN **$$**
(☑ 915-351-3677; www.cravekitchenandbar.com;
300 Cincinnati Ave; mains $11-28; ⊘ 7am-11pm
Mon-Sat, to 6pm Sun) Winning extra points
for style – from the cool sign to the cutlery
hanging from the ceiling – this hip little
eatery serves up creative comfort food:
green chilie mac 'n' cheese, juicy burgers
with sweet-potato waffle fries, and deca-
dent breakfasts. There's also a newer loca-
tion on the **east side** (☑ 915-594-7971; 11990
Rojas Dr).

⭐ **Cattleman's Steakhouse**   STEAK **$$$**
(☑ 915-544-3200; www.cattlemansranch.com; In-
dian Cliffs Ranch; mains $17-48; ⊘ 5-10pm Mon-Fri,
12:30-10pm Sat, 12:30-9pm Sun; ⛲) This place
is 20 miles east of the city, but local folks
would probably drive 200 miles to eat here.
The food is good, and the scenery is even
better. Portions are huge, and for just $6
extra you can share an entree and gain full
access to the family-style sides.

☆ Entertainment

Bars come and go quickly in El Paso.
Your best bet is to head to El Paso's mini-
entertainment district near the University
of Texas El Paso (around Cincinnati St between Mesa and Stanton) to see what's hap-
pening in the bars and restaurants that are
clustered there. Pick up the free weekly *El
Paso Scene* (www.epscene.com) or the Friday
'Tiempo' supplement to the *El Paso Times*
(www.elpasotimes.com) for cultural and music listings.

🔒 Shopping

On I-10 east of town, several warehouselike
shops sell all the goodies you can find in
Mexico – pottery, blankets, silver – at similar
prices.

El Paso Saddleblanket   SOUVENIRS
(☑ 915-544-1000; www.saddleblanket.com; 6926
Gateway Blvd E; ⊘ 9am-5pm Mon-Sat) 'Incredible
2-acre shopping adventure!' the billboards
scream. This place is indeed huge, and it's
chock-full of all things Southwestern. Stuff
your suitcases with pottery, blankets, turquoise jewelry, even a sombrero if you must.
They've got mounted steer horns, but we
can tell you right now you're not going to be
able to carry them onto the plane.

ℹ Information

El Paso Public Library (☑ 915-543-5433;
www.elpasolibrary.org; 501 N Oregon St;
⊘ 10am-7pm Mon-Thu, 11am-6pm Fri,
10am-6pm Sat, noon-6pm Sun; 🖥) Free internet access. Check the website for additional
branches.

El Paso Visitors Center (☑ 915-534-0600;
www.visitelpaso.com; 400 W San Antonio St;
⊘ 8am-5pm Mon-Fri, 9am-1pm Sat) Stocks
racks and racks of brochures, and the staff
is quite helpful. It also has a well-populated
website for planning.

❶ Getting There & Around

El Paso International Airport (ELP; www.elpaso internationalairport.com), 8 miles northeast of downtown off I-10, serves 16 US and two Mexican cities. Numerous chain rental-car companies are on site (you really need a car here).

Amtrak's Florida–California *Sunset Limited* stops at **Union Depot** (www.amtrak.com; 700 W San Francisco Ave). The terminal for **Greyhound** (www.greyhound.com; 200 W San Antonio Ave) is four blocks from the center of downtown.

Hueco Tanks State Historical Park

About 32 miles east of El Paso is the 860-acre Hueco Tanks State Historical Park (⦾ park 915-857-1135, reservations 512-389-8911; www.tpwd. state.tx.us; 6900 Hueco Tanks Rd/FM 2775; adult/child $7/free; ⊘ 8am-6pm). Popular today among rock climbers, the area has attracted humans for as many as 10,000 years, and park staff estimate there are more than 2000 pictographs at the site, some dating back 5000 years.

To minimize human impact, a daily visitor quota is enforced; make reservations 24 hours in advance to gain entry. You can explore the North Mountain area by yourself, but to hike deeper into the park – where the more interesting pictographs are – you have to reserve and join one of the pictograph, birding or hiking tours (⦾ 915-849-6684; tours per person $2) – call for the schedule.

Guadalupe Mountains National Park

We won't go so far as to call it Texas' best-kept secret, but the fact is that a lot of Texans aren't even aware of the Guadalupe Mountains National Park (⦾ 915-828-3251; www. nps.gov/gumo; US Hwy 62/180; 7-day pass adult/child under 16yr $5/free). It's just this side of the Texas–New Mexico state line and a long drive from practically everywhere in the state. Despite its low profile, it is a Texas high spot, both literally and figuratively. At 8749 ft, Guadalupe Peak is the highest point in the state.

The fall foliage in McKittrick Canyon is the best in west Texas, and more than half the park is a federally designated wilderness area.

The National Park Service has deliberately curbed development to keep the park wild. There are no restaurants or indoor accommodations and only a smattering of services and programs. But if you're looking for some of the best hiking and high-country

splendor Texas can muster, you should put this park on your itinerary.

Fort Davis & Around

False-front wooden buildings, an old fort and a stellar observatory make Texas' tallest town (elevation 5000ft) a Big Bend must-see. Its altitudinal advantage makes it a popular oasis during the summer, when west Texans head towards the mountains to escape the searing desert heat.

Of the towns in this region, Fort Davis is the closest to I-10. The main street through town is a stretch of Hwy 118 that's officially named State St, but everyone around here calls it Main St. The town is so small that, when you turn off Main St, you might well end up on a dirt road. Just a few miles west of town on Hwy 118 is Davis Mountains State Park.

◎ Sights & Activities

★ **McDonald Observatory**   OBSERVATORY
See p35, and below.

Fort Davis
National Historic Site   HISTORIC SITE
(⦾ 432-426-3224; www.nps.gov/foda; Hwy 17; adult/child $3/free; ⊘ 8am-5pm; ☻) A frontier military post with an impressive backdrop, Fort Davis was established in 1854 and abandoned in 1891. More than 20 buildings remain – five of them restored with period furnishings – as well as 100 or so ruins.

Davis Mountains State Park   PARK
(⦾ 432-426-3337; www.tpwd.state.tx.us; Hwy 118; adult/child under 12yr $6/free) Just a few miles northwest of Fort Davis on Hwy 118, set

BIG BEND & WEST TEXAS HUECO TANKS STATE HISTORICAL PARK

DON'T MISS

A STAR-STUDDED EVENT

On Tuesday, Friday and Saturday nights, about half an hour after sunset, McDonald Observatory shows off its favorite planets, galaxies and globular clusters at its popular Star Parties, where professional astronomers guide you in some heavy-duty stargazing. Using ridiculously powerful laser pointers, they give you a tour of the night sky, and you'll get to use some of the telescopes to play planetary Peeping Tom. (It gets surprisingly brisk up there at night, so dress warm and bring blankets.)

amid the most extensive mountain range in Texas, is Davis Mountains State Park. Hiking, mountain biking, horseback riding (BYO horse) and stargazing are all big attractions here, as is bird-watching. Pick up a bird checklist from park headquarters so you know what you're looking at, or, if you already know what you're looking at, use it to impress your bird-watching friends.

Davis Mountains Loop   SCENIC DRIVE, CYCLING
First you go up, up, up, then you come down, down, down. The countryside is so gorgeous, it's no wonder these 75 miles is considered one of the most scenic drives in the US. It's also tops among cyclists – at least, the ones who can handle the climb.

Take Hwy 118 northwest from town, then turn left on Hwy 166, which loops you back to town. Or go the opposite route; both afford equally appealing views, although the former is better in the morning so you're not driving or riding into the sun, while the latter is better in the afternoon.

🛏 Sleeping & Eating

Veranda Historic Inn   B&B $$
(☑888-383-2847; www.theveranda.com; 210 Court Ave; r $115-145; ❋ 🛜) A short stroll to the town center, this charming B&B has 10 antique-filled rooms and suites set in an 1883 adobe building. The oldest hotel in west Texas (hence the 'historic' namesake) has a shaded porch and pretty gardens – fine spots for a sundowner.

★**Indian Lodge**   INN $$
(☑lodge 432-426-3254, reservations 512-389-8982; Hwy 118; d $95-125, ste $150; ❋ 🛜 🏊) Located in the Davis Mountains State Park, this historic 39-room inn has 18in-thick adobe walls, hand-carved cedar furniture and ceilings of pine *viga* and *latilla* that give it the look of a Southwestern pueblo – that is, one with a swimming pool, gift shop and restaurant. The comfortable and surprisingly spacious guest rooms are a good value, so reserve early.

Fort Davis Drug Store   AMERICAN $$
(☑432-426-3118; www.fortdavisdrugstore.net; 113 N State St; mains $8-23; ⊙7am-9pm; 🛜🦽) Part diner, part old-fashioned soda fountain – but there's no 1950s nostalgia here. The theme is pure cowboy, with corrugated metal, big wooden chairs and lots of saddles providing the backdrop. Dine on country-style breakfasts, diner-style lunches and full meals at dinner. But whatever you do, save room for a banana split (or at least a milkshake).

Marfa

Founded in the 1880s Marfa got its first taste of fame when Rock Hudson, Elizabeth Taylor and James Dean came to town to film the 1956 Warner Brothers film *Giant*. It's also become a pilgrimage for art lovers, thanks to one of the world's largest installations of minimalist art. This, in turn, has attracted a disproportionate number of art galleries, quirky lodging options and interesting restaurants.

Marfa is on its own schedule, which is pretty much made up according to whim. Plan on coming late in the week or on a weekend; half the town is closed early in the week.

◉ Sights & Activities

Marfa has all sorts of art to explore, and you can pick up a list of galleries at the **Marfa Visitors Center** (☑432-729-4772; www.visit marfa.com; 302 S Highland Ave; ⊙9am-5pm Mon-Fri & event weekends).

Chinati Foundation Museum   MUSEUM
See p36.

Marfa Mystery Lights   PHENOMENON
Ghost lights, mystery lights...call them what you want, but the Marfa Lights that flicker beneath the Chinati Mountains have captured the imagination of many a traveler over the decades. On many nights, the mystery seems to be whether you're actually just seeing car headlights in the distance. Try your luck at the Marfa Lights Viewing Area about 9 miles east of Marfa on Hwy 90/67.

🎊 Festivals & Events

Every May or June, Marfa puts on the **Marfa Film Festival** (www.marfafilmfestival.org), screening features and shorts – including some of the Texas-centric films that have used Marfa as a location. And September brings the **Marfa Lights Festival** – which has little to do with the lights and is really just a good excuse to throw a town-wide street party.

🛏 Sleeping & Eating

★**El Cosmico**   CAMPGROUND $
(☑432-729-1950; www.elcosmico.com; 802 S Highland Ave; tent sites per person $15, safari tents $85-100, teepees $90-150, trailers $120-185, yurt $150; 🛜) One of the funkiest choices in all of Texas, El Cosmico lets you sleep in a stylishly converted travel trailer, a teepee, a safari tent – or even a yurt. It's not for everyone: the grounds are dry and dusty, you might have to

DETOUR: BALMORHEA STATE PARK

Swimming, scuba diving and snorkeling are the attractions at the 46-acre Balmorhea State Park (📞432-375-2370; www.tpwd.state.tx.us; Hwy 17; adult/under 12yr $7/free; ⏱8am-sunset), a true oasis in the west Texas desert. The swimming pool covers 1.75 acres, making it the largest spring-fed swimming facility in the US; it's 25ft deep and about 75°F year-round. The park is at Toyahvale, 5 miles south of the town of Balmorhea (pronounced bal-mo-ray), which itself is just off I-10.

shower outdoors, and there's no AC (luckily, it's cool at night). But, hey, how often do you get to sleep in a Kozy Coach?

Thunderbird BOUTIQUE HOTEL $$
(📞877-729-1984; www.thunderbirdmarfa.com; 601 W San Antonio St; d $140-190; ❄🛜☕) This classic 1950s motel was reopened in 2005 as a small boutique with a spiffy new look. The rooms are hip and minimalist, and the grounds and common areas are as cool as the desert air at night.

Hotel Paisano HOTEL $$
(📞432-729-3669; www.hotelpaisano.com; 207 N Highland Ave; d $100-150, ste $160-260; ❄@🛜☕) Marfa's historic hotel has a unique claim to fame: it's where the cast of the movie *Giant* stayed. The comfy rooms are nicely designed, and the whole place does have a dignified charm. The best rooms have a fireplace and a private terrace. There's a first-rate restaurant (Jett's), a snazzy covered pool and a touch of taxidermy for good measure.

Food Shark FOOD TRAILER $
(www.foodsharkmarfa.com; 222 W San Antonio St; mains $5-8; ⏱noon-3pm Fri-Sun) See that battered old food trailer near the main road through town? If you do, that means Food Shark is open for business. If you're lucky enough to catch them, you'll find incredibly fresh Greek salad and their specialty, the Marfalafel. Daily specials are excellent, and sell out early.

Squeeze Marfa CAFE $
(📞432-729-4500; www.squeezemarfa.com; 215 N Highland Ave; mains $5-10; ⏱8am-3pm Tue-Sun; 🛜) This cute little cafe across from the courthouse serves fresh and healthy breakfasts, lunches and smoothies, all the better to enjoy on the narrow, shady patio. The address is on Highland, but the entrance is on Lincoln.

★**Cochineal** AMERICAN $$$
(📞432-729-3300; cochinealmarfa.com; 107 W San Antonio St; small plates $8-14, mains around $26; ⏱9am-1pm Sun, 5:30-10pm Thu-Tue) Foodies

flock to this stylish but minimalist eatery (with outdoor courtyard) for a changing menu that showcases high-quality organic ingredients. Portions are generous, so don't be afraid to share a few small plates (along the lines of brisket tacos, oyster mushroom risotto and housemade ramen with duck breast) in lieu of a full dinner. Reservations are recommended.

🍷 Drinking & Nightlife

★**Planet Marfa** BAR
(📞432-386-5099; 200 S Abbott St; ⏱2pm-midnight Fri & Sat, to 7pm Sun) Nightlife, Marfa style, is epitomized in this wonderfully funky open-air bar. There's usually live music at night, and shelters are scattered about to protect you from the elements. If you're lucky, someone will save you a spot inside the teepee.

Lost Horse BAR
(www.losthorsesaloon.com; 306 E San Antonio St; ⏱4pm-midnight) Follow the crack of pool balls and the crooning of a solitary country-and-western singer to this atmospheric cowboy bar on the main strip. It has saddles and skulls, taxidermy and an eye-patch-wearing owner named Ty Mitchell. Thirsty folk shouldn't miss this Texas classic writ large.

Alpine

Primarily a pit stop, this university town has no real attractions of note. But it has the most sizable population (5700) in Big Bend – and is the only place with big-name chain motels, numerous restaurants, grocery stores and more than one gas station. You can get region-wide information at the Alpine Chamber of Commerce (📞432-837-2326; www.alpinetexas.com; 106 N 3rd St; ⏱9am-5pm Mon-Fri, to 4pm Sat).

Museum of the Big Bend MUSEUM
(📞432-837-8143; www.museumofthebigbend.com; 400 N Harrison St; donations accepted; ⏱9am-5pm Tue-Sat, 1-5pm Sun) FREE On the

Boquillas Canyon Trail (p38), Big Bend National Park
DAVID NEVALA / GETTY IMAGES ©

campus of Sul Ross State University, this little museum is a great place to delve into the past, with exhibits on marine fossils (a warm shallow sea covered Big Bend 135 million years ago), Native American pictographs, Spanish missionaries, Mexican pioneers, buffalo soldiers (a nickname for the African American soldiers who fought in the Civil War) and of course cowboys (with a full-scale chuck wagon on display).

Hancock Hill VIEWPOINT
(E Ave B) Behind Sul Ross State University a trail leads up the dusty slopes of Hancock Hill. There are fine views of the area and some curious artifacts here – including a battered desk that some uni students dragged here back in 1981. To reach the desk, head uphill to the first rock pile and follow the trail to the right. It's about a 20-minute walk.

🛏 Sleeping & Eating

Antelope Lodge CABIN $
(☑ 432-837-2451; www.antelopelodge.com; 2310 W Hwy 90; s $53-75, d $58-80, ste $105-120; 🌡 🛜 🐾) You'd think from the name you were getting a hunting lodge, but it's nothing like that. Rustic stucco cottages with Spanish-tile roofs – each one holding two guest rooms – sit sprinkled about a shady lawn. There's a casual, pleasant vibe, and the rooms have kitchenettes. Ask the geologically minded owner about guided rock hunts.

★ Holland Hotel HISTORIC HOTEL $$
(☑ 432-837-3844; www.thehollandhoteltexas. com; 209 W Holland Ave; d $105-125, ste $140-220; 😑 🌡 🛜 🐾) Built in 1928 this beautifully renovated Spanish Colonial building has elegantly furnished rooms set with carved wood furniture, Western-style artwork and sleek modern bathrooms. The lobby, with its stuffed leather chairs and wood-beamed ceiling, is a classy setting in which to unwind. There's a good high-end restaurant attached.

Maverick Inn MOTEL $$
(☑ 432-837-0628; www.themaverickinn.com; 1200 E Holland Ave; r $106-125; 🌡 🛜 🐾 🐾) The maverick road-tripper will feel right at home at this retro motor court that's been smartly renovated to include luxury bedding and flat-screen TVs. Rooms have Texas-style furnishings and terracotta floors, and the pool looks mighty nice after a hot, dusty day. You can also borrow a guitar or peruse the Texas coffee-table books in the lobby.

Magoo's AMERICAN $
(905 E Ave East; mains $4-10; ⏰ 6am-2pm Mon-Fri, 7am-noon Sat & Sun) A no-fuss diner that's always packed, Magoo's is the go-to spot for breakfast burritos, huevos rancheros, pancakes and other breakfast fare.

★ Reata STEAK $$
(☑ 432-837-9232; www.reata.net; 203 N 5th St; lunch mains $9-17, dinner $16-25; ⏰ 11:30am-2pm & 5-10pm Mon-Sat) Named after the ranch in the movie *Giant*, Reata does turn on the upscale ranch-style charm – at least in the front dining room, where the serious diners go. Step back into the lively bar area or onto the shady patio and it's a completely different vibe, where you can feel free to nibble your way around the menu and enjoy a margarita.

Marathon

One of Marathon's claims to fame, the Gage Hotel (p37), has a fabulous Old West style that's matched only by its love of taxidermy. Each room at this property is individually (though similarly) decorated with Native American blankets, cowboy gear and leather accents. The associated 12 Gage (☑432-386-4205; 101 US 90 W; mains $20-45; ⏰6-9pm Sun-Thu, to 10pm Fri & Sat) whips up gourmet renditions of Texas faves, and the White Buffalo Bar (☑432-386-4205; 101 US 90 W; ⏰4pm-midnight Sun-Thu, 3pm-2am Fri & Sat) invites you to enjoy a margarita while trying to ignore its namesake's glassy stare.

Before heading to Big Bend, stock up on picnic supplies at French Co. Grocer (☑432-386-4522; www.frenchcogrocer.com; 206 N Ave D; ☉7:30am-9pm Mon-Fri, from 8am Sat, from 9am Sun), or enjoy them at the tables outside at this charming little grocery – formerly the WM French General Merchandise store, established in 1900.

Big Bend National Park

Everyone knows Texas is huge. But you can't really appreciate just how big it is until you visit this national park (p37). Despite its sprawl, Big Bend is laced with enough well-placed roads and trails to permit short-term visitors to see a lot in two to three days.

Like many popular US parks, Big Bend has one area – the Chisos Basin – that absorbs the overwhelming crunch of traffic. But any visit should also include time in the Chihuahuan Desert, home to curious creatures and adaptable plants, and the Rio Grande, a watery border between the US and Mexico.

🏃 Activities

Scenic Drives

With 110 miles of paved road and 150 miles of dirt road, scenic driving is easily the park's most popular activity. Booklets are available for $1.95 from the visitor centers to help you make the most of it.

Maverick Drive The 22-mile stretch between the west entrance and park headquarters is notable for its desert scenery and wildlife. Just west of Basin Junction, a side trip on the gravel Grapevine Hills Rd leads to fields of oddly shaped boulders.

Ross Maxwell Scenic Drive This 30-mile route leaves Maverick Dr midway between the west entrance and park headquarters. The Chisos Mountains provide a grand panorama, and the big payoff is the view of Santa Elena Canyon and its sheer rock walls.

Rio Grande Village Drive This 20-mile drive leads from park headquarters toward the Sierra del Carmen range, running through the park toward Mexico. The best time to take this drive is at sunrise or sunset, when the mountains glow brilliantly with different hues.

River Trips

The Rio Grande has earned its place among the top North American river trips for both rafting and canoeing. Rapids up to class IV alternate with calm stretches that are perfect for wildlife viewing, photography and just plain relaxation.

Trips on the river can range from several hours to several days. Boquillas Canyon is the longest and most tranquil of the park's three canyons and is best for intermediate to advanced boaters and canoeists with camping skills. Colorado Canyon is just upriver from the park and, depending on the water level, has lots of white water. Mariscal Canyon is noted for its beauty and isolation, and Santa Elena Canyon is a classic float featuring the class IV Rock Slide rapid.

Guided floats cost about $140 per person per day, $80 for a half day, including all meals and gear (except a sleeping bag for overnighters). These three companies have been in business a long time and have solid reputations:

Big Bend River Tours (☑800-545-4240; www.bigbendrivertours.com; Rte 170, Terlingua) offers saddle-paddle tours with half a day each rowing and horseback riding.

Desert Sports (☑888-989-6900; www.desert sportstx.com; Rte 170, Terlingua) is tops with bikers for its bike-canoe combo trips.

Far Flung Adventures (☑800-839-7238; www.bigbendfarflung.com; Terlingua) puts together fun outings such as a wine-tasting river trip.

Want to go it alone? Any of the above companies will rent you equipment and provide shuttle service. Just remember to obtain your free permit at Panther Junction within

---

BOQUILLAS: CROSSING THE RIO GRANDE INTO MEXICO

For years, one of the added draws of Big Bend was crossing the Rio Grande into the quaint Mexican village of Boquillas. After more than a decade of closure, the border has again opened to visitors. A boat will take you across ($5 return); once on the other side you can hire a burro ($8 return), walk or take a truck for the 1 mile to Boquillas village. There you need to get stamped in at the Mexican immigration office. You can have lunch, peruse local handicrafts and wander around the town before heading back to the river (leave by 5pm to avoid getting stranded). The border opens from 9am to 6pm Wednesday to Sunday. You'll need your passport. Check https://discover boquillas.wordpress.com for more info.

24 hours before putting in. Permits for the lower canyons of the Rio Grande are available at the Persimmon Gap visitor center and the Stillwell Store on FM 2627.

Sleeping & Eating

In the heart of the park, Chisos Mountains Lodge (432-477-2291; www.chisosmountains lodge.com; lodge & motel r $156, cottages $174;) offers lodging in the sought-after Roosevelt Stone Cottages or in one of two motel-style lodges. There's also a dining room (Lodge Dining Room; Chisos Mountains Lodge; mains $10-24; 7-10am, 11am-4pm & 5-8pm) within the complex, as well as a camp store (432-477-2291; 8am-9pm) with basic supplies.

For tent campers or smaller RVs that don't require hookups, there are three main campgrounds, some of which can be reserved, some of which are first-come, first-served. When everything's full, rangers direct tent campers to primitive sites throughout the Big Bend backcountry. Most popular – thanks to its mountain climate – is the Chisos Basin Campground (877-444-6777; www.recreation. gov; campsites $14).

Information

Get the scoop on the most popular hikes at the Panther Junction Visitors Center (432-477-2251; 9am-5pm) on the main park road, 29 miles south of the northern Persimmon Gap entrance and 26 miles east of the Maverick entrance at Study Butte.

West of Big Bend National Park

Small towns. Ghost towns. Towns that aren't even really towns. Throw in lots of dust and a scorching summer heat that dries out the stream of visitors until it's just a trickle. This isn't everyone's idea of a dream vacation. But if you can't relax out here, then you just plain can't relax. Whatever concerns you in your everyday life is likely to melt away along with anything you leave in your car.

Terlingua

A mining boomtown in the late 19th and early 20th centuries, Terlingua went bust when the mines were closed down in the 1940s. The town dried up and blew away like a tumbleweed, leaving buildings that fell into ruins and earning Terlingua a place in Texas folklore as a ghost town. But slowly the area has become repopulated, thanks in large part to the fact that it's only a few miles outside of Big Bend National Park.

By the way, you'll hear people talk about Terlingua, Study Butte and Terlingua ghost town as if they're three different towns, but the only real town here is Terlingua; the other two are just areas of the town. Addresses are a relative and fluid thing out here; have patience if you're using a GPS, but take comfort in knowing the town's not all that big.

Roadside sculpture near Terlingua

🛏 Sleeping & Eating

Chisos Mining Co Motel MOTEL **$**
(☑ 432-371-2254; www.cmcm.cc; 23280 FM 170;
s/d/cabins $60/79/101; ❄) You'll recognize
this quirky little place less than a mile west
of Hwy 118 when you spot the oversize Easter eggs on the roof. The rooms are minimalist but as cheap as you'll find.

★ **La Posada Milagro** INN **$$**
(☑ 432-371-3044; www.laposadamilagro.net; 100
Milagro Rd; d $185-210; ❄🤖) Built on top of
and even incorporating some of the adobe
ruins of the historic ghost town, this guest-
house pulls off the amazing feat of providing
stylish rooms that blend in perfectly with the
surroundings. The decor is west-Texas chic,
and there's a nice patio for enjoying the cool
evenings.

Espresso...Y Poco Mas CAFE **$**
(☑ 432-371-3044; 100 Milagro Rd; snacks $3-7;
⊙8am-2pm; 🤖) We love this friendly lit-
tle walk-up counter at La Posada Milagro,
where you can find pastries, breakfast burri-
tos, lunches and what might just be the best
iced coffee in all of west Texas.

★ **Starlight Theater** AMERICAN **$$**
See p38.

🔒 Shopping

Terlingua Trading Co GIFTS
(☑ 432-371-2234; www.ghosttowntexas.com/ter
linguatradingcompany.html; 100 Ivey St; ⊙10am-
8pm) This store in the ghost town has
great gifts, from hot sauces and wines to
an impressive selection of books. Pick up a
brochure on the walking tour of historic
Terlingua, or buy a beer inside the store and
hang out on the porch with locals at sunset.

Lajitas to Presidio

About half an hour west from the junction in
Terlingua, you can trade funky and dusty for
trendy and upscale (but still dusty) at **Lajitas
Golf Resort & Spa** (☑ 432-424-5000; www.laji
tasgolfresort.com; d from $180; ❄❄🤖❄❄).
What used to be small-town Texas got bought
up and revamped into a swanky destination.
The old Trading Post is gone and in its place
is a new general store. (The former Trading
Post was the stuff of folk legend, as it was the
home of a beer-drinking goat who got elect-
ed mayor of the town. Alas, no more.)

The nine-hole golf course that included a
shot over the river into Mexico has moved to

SCENIC DRIVE: RIVER ROAD

West of Lajitas, Rte 170 (also known as
River Rd, or *El Camino Del Rio* in Spanish)
hugs the Rio Grande through some of the
most spectacular and remote scenery in
Big Bend country. Relatively few Big Bend
visitors experience this driving adventure,
even though it can be navigated in any
vehicle with good brakes. Strap in and
hold on: you have the Rio Grande on one
side and fanciful geological formations
all around, and at one point there's a 15%
grade – the maximum allowable. When
you reach Presidio, head north on US 67
to get to Marfa. Or, if you plan to go back
the way you came, at least travel as far as
Colorado Canyon (20 miles from Lajitas)
for the best scenery.

drier ground to escape flooding, and now it's
the 18-hole Black Jack's Crossing. **Lajitas
Stables** (☑ 432-371-2212; www.lajitasstables.
com; Rte 170; 2hr rides $75) offers short horse-
back trail rides as well as full-day rides to the
Buena Suerte Mine and Ghost Town.

Lajitas is the eastern gateway of the
massive **Big Bend Ranch State Park**
(☑ 432-358-4444; www.tpwd.state.tx.us; off Rte
170; adult peak/nonpeak $5/3, child under 12yr free).
At 433 sq miles, it's more than 11 times larger
than Texas' next biggest state park (Franklin Mountains in El Paso). Taking up almost
all the desert between Lajitas and Presidio,
Big Bend Ranch reaches north from the Rio
Grande into some of the wildest country in
North America. It is full of notable features,
most prominently the Solitario, formed 36
million years ago in a volcanic explosion.
The resulting caldera measures 8 miles east
to west and 9 miles north to south. As massive as it is, this former ranch is one of the
best-kept secrets in Big Bend country.

Access to the park is limited and a permit is
required, even if you're just passing through.
Coming from Lajitas, stop at the **Barton
Warnock Visitor Center** (☑ 432-424-3327;
www.tpwd.state.tx.us; FM 170; ⊙8am-4:30pm daily)
for your day-use and camping permits (primitive campsites $8, backcountry $5). This ed-
ucation center is staffed by some of the most
knowledgeable folks in the region. On the
western edge of the park, you can pick up a
permit at the **Fort Leaton State Historic
Site** (☑ 432-229-3613; FM 170; ⊙8am-4:30pm), a
restored adobe fortress.

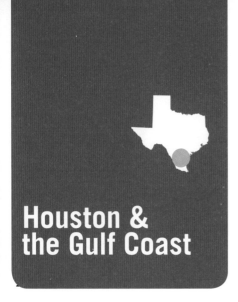

Known for its sparkling bays, small harbors and protected beaches, the Gulf Coast is littered with tiny coastal communities and wandering coastal back roads – reason enough to visit.

Houston & the Gulf Coast

Houston

Concrete superhighways may blind you to Houston's good points when you first zoom into this sprawling city. You'll miss out if you limit yourself to downtown: diverse residential neighborhoods and enclaves of restaurants and shops are spread far and wide.

The leafy Museum District is the city's cultural center; Upper Kirby and River Oaks have upscale shopping and dining; Montrose contains cute bungalows, quirky shops and eateries; Midtown has up-and-coming condos and some good restaurants; Washington Ave is nightlife central; and the Heights has historic homes and boutiques.

⊙ Sights & Activities

Museum lovers will find plenty to love in the area north of Hermann Park. To get a full list of options or to plot your route, check out the map on the Houston Museum District (www.houstonmuseumdistrict.org) website.

A couple of the city's main attractions – NASA's Space Center Houston in Clear Lake and Galveston Island – are outside the city limits, requiring a 45-minute drive down I-45.

★**Menil Collection**   MUSEUM
(www.menil.org; 1515 Sul Ross St; ⊙11am-7pm Wed-Sun) **FREE** The late local philanthropists John and Dominique de Menil collected more than 17,000 paintings, drawings, sculptures, archaeological artifacts and more during their lives. The modernist building, designed by Renzo Piano, houses rotating highlights from the collection – everything from 5000-year-old antiquities to works by Kara Walker and today's art stars – plus rotating exhibitions. Don't forget to also saunter over to the Cy Twombly Gallery and the highly meditative Rothko Chapel, annexes of the collection.

Museum of Fine Arts Houston   MUSEUM
(www.mfah.org; 1001 Bissonnet St; adult/teen/child $15/7.50/free; ⊙10am-5pm Tue & Wed, to 9pm Thu, to 7pm Fri & Sat, 12:15-7pm Sun; Ⓜ Mu

---

AND NOW FOR SOMETHING COMPLETELY DIFFERENT

Conservative Houston has a wacky creative streak, especially when it comes to its quirkiest museums. Follow up a visit to the Art Car Museum with a pilgrimage to the Orange Show Center for Visionary Art (☎713-926-6368; www.orangeshow.org; 2402 Munger St; adult/child $5/2; ⊙10am-2pm Wed-Sun), a mazelike junk-art tribute to one man's favorite citrus fruit. The center fosters the folk-art vision by offering children's art education and keeping up the 50,000-strong Beer Can House (www.beercanhouse.org; 222 Malone St, off Memorial Dr; adult/child $5/2; ⊙noon-5pm Sat & Sun).

seum District) French impressionism and post-1945 European and American painting really shine in this nationally renowned palace of art, which includes major works by Picasso and Rembrandt. Across the street, admire the talents of luminaries such as Rodin and Matisse in the associated Cullen Sculpture Garden (cnr Montrose Blvd & Bissonnet St; ⊙ dawn to dusk) FREE.

Art Car Museum MUSEUM
(www.artcarmuseum.com; 140 Heights Blvd; ⊙ 11am-6pm Wed-Sun) FREE The handful of art cars represented here are something to behold; some of them are straight out of *Mad Max*. But they're really just bait to lure you in to check out the quirky-cool rotating art exhibits, which have included subjects such as road refuse and bone art.

⭐ Festivals & Events

Houston Livestock Show & Rodeo RODEO
(www.rodeohouston.com) For three weeks beginning in late February or early March, rodeo fever takes over Houston. The barbecue cook-off is a hot seller, but so are the nightly rodeos followed by big-name concerts – featuring stars from Bruno Mars to Blake Shelton. Buy tickets way in advance. Fairgrounds-only admission gets you access to midway rides, livestock shows, shopping and nightly dances.

Art Car Parade & Festival PARADE
(www.thehoustonartcarparade.com) Wacky, arted-out vehicles (think *Mad Max* or giant rabbits) hit the streets en masse on the second Saturday of April. The parade itself is complemented by weekend-long festivities, including concerts.

🛏 Sleeping

Chain motels line all the major freeways. If you are visiting the Space Center and Galveston, consider staying on I-45 south.

Morty Rich Hostel HOSTEL $
(☎ 713-636-9776; www.hiusa.org/houston; 501 Lovett Blvd; dm $26-32, d $80; P ❈ @ 🛜 🛉) A beautiful Montrose mansion (a previous mayor's residence) hosts this plush Hosteling International member. The rooms are bright and clean, with four to eight rickety beds per dorm, many with ensuite. There's also one private double (book well ahead). Hang out in the billiard room or cool off in the backyard pool after a hard day's sightseeing. Accessible via public transport.

HOUSTON, WE HAVE AN ATTRACTION...

Dream of a landing on the moon? You can't get any closer (without years of training) than at Space Center Houston (☎ 281-244-2100; http://spacecenter.org; 1601 NASA Pkwy 1; with audio guide adult/child $24/19; ⊙ 10am-5pm Mon-Fri, to 7pm Sat & Sun), off I-45 S, the official visitor center and museum of NASA's Johnson Space Center. Interactive exhibits let you try your hand at picking up an object in space or landing the shuttle. Be sure to enter the theater that shows short films, because you exit past *Apollo* capsules and history exhibits. The free tram tour covers the center at work – shuttle training facilities, zero-gravity labs and the original mission control, from which was uttered the famous words, 'Houston, we have a problem.'

Modern B&B B&B $$
(☎ 832-279-6367; http://modernbb.com; 4003 Hazard St; r incl breakfast $100-225; P ❈ @ 🛜) 🌿 An architect's dream, this mod, 11-room inn is rife with airy decks, spiral staircases and sunlight. Think organic mattresses, in-room Jacuzzi tubs, private decks and iPod docking stations. Owners also rent out several nearby apartments.

Sara's Inn on the Boulevard INN $$
(☎ 713-868-1130; www.saras.com; 941 Heights Blvd; r incl breakfast $130-200; P ❈ @ 🛜) A Queen Anne Victorian feels right at home among the historic houses of the Heights. Eleven airy rooms say 'boutique hotel' more than 'frilly B&B.' But the inn still has the kind of sprawling Southern porch that makes you want to gossip over mint juleps.

⭐ Hotel ZaZa BOUTIQUE HOTEL $$$
(☎ 713-526-1991; www.hotelzaza.com; 5701 Main St; r $250-295; P ❈ @ 🛜 🛉; M Hermann Park/Rice) Hip, flamboyant and fabulous. From the bordello-esque colors to zebra accent chairs, everything about Hotel ZaZa is good fun – and surprisingly unpretentious. Our favorite rooms are the concept suites such as the eccentric Geisha House, or the space-age 'Houston We Have a Problem.' You can't beat the location overlooking the Museum District's Hermann Park, near the light rail.

Map with labels including:

Ella Lee La, Reba Dr, Locke La, Westheimer Rd, Westgate Dr, S Shepherd Dr, Brun St, Hazard St, Morse St, Park St, Fairview St, Rudyard's Pub (0.2mi), Art Car Museum (2mi), California St, Lovett Blvd, MONTROSE, Kipling St, Argonne, Revere, Persa, Kipling St, Woodhead St, Hawthorne St, Harold St, Kipling St, Marshall St, Mulberry St, Yupon Dr, Graustark St, Mt Vernon St, Yoakum Blvd, Roseland St, Stanford St, W Alabama St, UPPER KIRBY, Sul Ross St, Greenbriar Dr, Branard St, W Main, Menil Collection, Branard St, Sul Ross St, Branard St, W Main St, Colquitt St, W Main St, Colquitt St, Greeley St, Portsmouth St, Norfolk St, Richmond Ave, Dunlavy St, Bonnie Brae St, Kyle St, Norfolk St, Lexington St, Dunlavy Park, Southwest Fwy, Vassar St, Autrey St, Montrose Blvd, Kirby Dr, Greenbriar Dr, Banks St, Milford St, North Blvd, South Blvd, Milford St, North Blvd, Baynard St, Museum District, Dincans St, Bartlett, Bissonnet St, Woodhead St, Dora St, Albans Rd, Kelvin Dr, Morningside Dr, Wroxton Rd, Kent St, Ashby St, Cherokee St, Remington Ln, San Jacinto St, Robinhood Rd, Sunset Blvd, Tangley St, Hazard St, Wilton St, Sunset, Fordham St, Lake St, Dunstan Rd, Rice Blvd, S Shepherd Dr, Loop Rd, Rice University, Hermann Park Dr, Fannin St, Zoo Circle Dr, Shakespeare St, Dryden Rd, Barbara Swift Blvd, Addison Rd, Stockton Dr, Main St, University Blvd, Dryden Rd

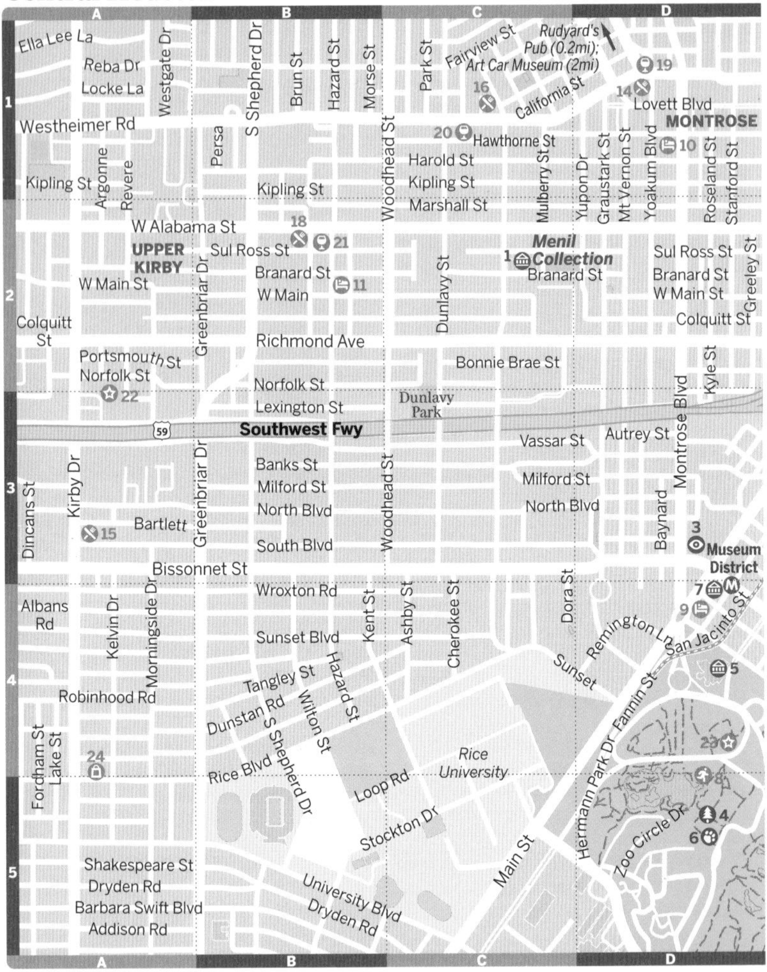

✗ Eating

Houston's restaurant scene is smokin' hot – and we don't just mean the salsa. In fact, Houstonians eat out more than residents of any other US city. To keep abreast of what's in and what isn't, we recommend the razor-tongued Fearless Critic (www.fearlesscritic.com). Twitterites can follow @eatdrinkhouston.

Tacos Tierra Caliente   MEXICAN $
(1919 W Alabama St; tacos $2; ⊙9am-11pm) By our reckoning, these are the best tacos in the city, and thousands of Houstonians agree. They're served piled high from a battered food truck, and although there's nowhere

to sit, just across the road is the West Alabama Ice House (☑713-528-6874; 1919 W Alabama St; ⊙10am-midnight Mon-Fri, to 1am Sat, noon-midnight Sun); a fine spot for a taco feast while nursing a few cold ones.

Breakfast Klub   SOUTHERN $
(www.thebreakfastklub.com; 3711 Travis St; mains $9-16; ⊙7am-2pm Mon-Fri, 8am-2pm Sat & Sun; ℗🛜) Come early; devotees line up around the block for down-home breakfast faves like fried wings 'n' waffles. Lunch hours are only slightly less crazy at this coffeehouselike eatery favored by local girl Beyonce, and her boy Jay-Z. Coffee is great and there's wi-fi.

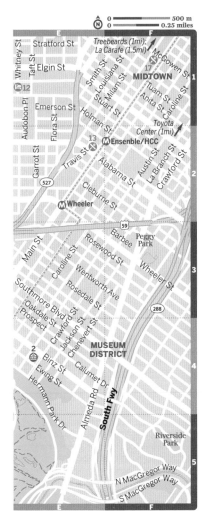

Central Houston

◎ **Top Sights**
1 Menil Collection......................................C2

◎ **Sights**
2 Children's Museum of Houston..........E4
3 Cullen Sculpture Garden D3
4 Hermann Park......................................D5
5 Houston Museum of Natural
   Science... D4
6 Houston Zoo...D5
7 Museum of Fine Arts Houston D4

◎ **Activities, Courses & Tours**
8 Hermann Park Miniature Train D5

◎ **Sleeping**
9 Hotel ZaZa D4
10 La Colombe d'Or Hotel....................... D1
11 Modern B&B...B2
12 Morty Rich Hostel................................E1

◎ **Eating**
13 Breakfast Klub.....................................E2
14 El Real D1
15 Goode Co BBQ.....................................A3
16 Hugo's C1
17 Reef..F1
   Sparrow Bar & Cookshop.........(see 13)
18 Tacos Tierra Caliente.........................B2

◎ **Drinking & Nightlife**
19 Hay Merchant D1
20 Poison Girl..C1
21 West Alabama Ice House....................B2

◎ **Entertainment**
22 McGonigel's Mucky Duck A3
23 Miller Outdoor Theatre D4

◎ **Shopping**
24 Rice Village A4

chips precede every order, which you can nibble while watching old Westerns (no sound) projected onto the back wall.

Treebeards SOUTHERN $
(http://treebeards.com; 315 Travis St; mains $8-12; ⊙11am-2:30pm Mon-Fri) Locals flock here at lunchtime to chow down on savory Cajun gumbos and crawfish étoufée, but don't discount the appeal of daily changing specials like jerk chicken and blackened catfish.

El Real TEX-MEX $$
(1201 Westheimer Rd; mains $10-24; ⊙11am-10pm Sun-Thu, to midnight Fri & Sat) Set in a former movie theater, El Real serves up first-rate Tex-Mex, with sizzling fajitas, steaming enchiladas and fluffy soft-shelled tacos among many standout choices. Warm salsa and

Original Ninfas MEXICAN $$
(www.ninfas.com; 2704 Navigation Blvd; mains $11-24; ⊙11am-10pm Mon-Fri, 10am-10pm Sat & Sun) Generations of Houstonians have come here since the 1970s for shrimp diablo, *tacos al carbon* (tacos cooked over charcoal) and handmade tamales crafted with pride.

Reef SEAFOOD $$
(☎713-526-8282; www.reefhouston.com; 2600 Travis St; lunch mains $10-30, dinner $22-36; ⊙11am-10pm Mon-Fri, 5-11pm Sat; Ⓜ McGowen) Gulf Coast seafood is creatively prepared and served in a sleek dining room. Chef Bryan Caswell has won oodles of national awards for himself and his restaurant.

Goode Co BBQ
BARBECUE **$$**
(www.goodecompany.com; 5109 Kirby Dr; plates $11-17; ⊘11am-10pm) Belly up to the beef brisket, smoked sausage and gallon ice teas in a big ol' barn or out back on picnic tables.

★ Hugo's
MEXICAN **$$$**
(☎713-524-7744; http://hugosrestaurant.net; 1600 Westheimer Rd; lunch mains $15-22, dinner $23-30; ⊘11am-10pm Mon-Thu, 11am-11pm Fri & Sat, 10am-9pm Sun) Chef Hugo Ortega elevates regional Mexican cooking and street food to high art in this much celebrated Montrose gem. You can sample Oaxacan-style *tlayuda* (huge corn tortilla with cheese and skirt steak), *tikin xic* (achiote-rubbed grouper with jicama salad), or nibble on sauteed *chapulines* (grasshoppers). Brunch is outstanding. Book ahead for any meal.

Sparrow Bar & Cookshop
MODERN AMERICAN **$$$**
(☎713-524-6922; http://sparrowhouston.com; 3701 Travis St; mains $16-32; ⊘10am-3pm & 5-11pm Tue-Sat; ✎) Nationally renowned chef Monica Pope brings top-quality local and organic ingredients to life in her New American cuisine. Share plates might include bacon-wrapped dates stuffed with chorizo, mushroom dumplings with a blue cheese sauce, or vegetable dal. On a nice night, patio dining is a must.

Drinking & Nightlife
To the youngish set, the stretch of Washington Ave bars and clubs defines all that is hip and happening in Houston nightlife (although lately downtown is none too shabby in that department). The corner of White Oak Dr and Studemont St in the Heights has a few funky little bars, including a roadhouse, a tiki bar and a live-music club in an old house.

★ La Carafe
BAR
(813 Congress St; ⊘1pm-2am) Set in Houston's oldest building, La Carafe is the most atmospheric bar in the city. It's a warmly lit drinking den, with exposed brick, sepia photos on the walls and flickering candles. You'll also find a great jukebox and a friendly eclectic crowd. On weekends the upstairs bar room opens, with a 2nd floor balcony overlooking Market Square.

Bad News Bar
COCKTAIL BAR
(2nd fl, 308 Main St; ⊘5pm-2am) On restaurant-lined Main St, look for the door marked with law offices, then ascend the stairs to this elegant cocktail den. Take a seat at the long polished bar, or in an armchair beneath low-lit chandeliers, and sip some of Hou-

ston's finest libations. On warm nights the inviting terrace over the street is a perfect spot to enjoy the night air.

Onion Creek Cafe
CAFE
(3106 White Oak Dr; ⊘7am-midnight Sun-Wed, 7 to 2am Thu-Sat) Open for early-morning coffee and breakfast tacos through to late-night cocktails and house-smoked brisket sliders, Onion Creek is the quintessential hangout in the Heights. On weekends every table on the sprawling, tree-filled patio is taken.

Hay Merchant
BAR
(haymerchant.com; 1100 Westheimer Rd, Montrose; ⊘3pm-2am Mon-Fri, from 11am Sat & Sun) This wildly popular gastropub has a dazzling selection of craft beers from around the globe on draft, with everything from easy-drinking Belgian-style ales to malty imperial stouts. Creative and delicious bar food (housemade wagyu beef jerky, fried pig ears) seals the deal. It has an industrial design and a small outdoor patio.

☆ Entertainment
There's a fair bit of nightlife around the Preston and Main St Sq Metro Rail stops downtown. Montrose and Midtown have clubs, but they're spread around. Look for listings in the independent weekly *Houston Press* (www.houstonpress.com) and in the Thursday edition of the *Houston Chronicle* (www.chron.com).

For theater and performing arts, the Houston Grand Opera, the Society of the Performing Arts, Houston Ballet, Da Camera chamber orchestra and the Houston Symphony all perform downtown in the Theater District (www.houstontheaterdistrict.org). From the district's website, you can purchase tickets and view all schedules.

Rudyard's Pub
LIVE MUSIC
(☎713-521-0521; www.rudyards.com; 2010 Waugh Dr; ⊘11:30am-2am) Host to unusual fare (grown-up storytime, punk comedy), plus a mix of experimental and indie bands, Rudyard's is a reliable spot for a fun night out. A great selection of microbrews and good pub grub (especially the burgers).

McGonigel's Mucky Duck
LIVE MUSIC
(☎713-528-5999; www.mcgonigels.com; 2425 Norfolk St; ⊘11am-11pm Mon-Thu, to 2am Fri & Sat, 5:30-9pm Sun) Acoustic, Irish, folk and country performers play nightly in pubby surrounds. Concert prices vary – typically running $22 to $30 – but Mondays (open-mike) and Wednes-

days (Irish folk) are free. It's a great space with a classy supper-club look, and nicely prepared pub food.

Last Concert Cafe   LIVE MUSIC
(☑713-226-8563; www.lastconcert.com; 1403 Nance St; ☺11am-2am Tue-Sat, 10:30am-10pm Sun) For a real local original, find your way to the warehouse district northeast of downtown. After you knock on the red door (there's no sign), you can hang out drinking frothy suds at the bar or dig into cheap Tex-Mex and listen to live music in the grassy, palm-filled backyard.

Reliant Stadium   FOOTBALL
(www.reliantpark.com; 1 Reliant Park) The Houston Texans (www.houstontexans.com) play at this high-tech stadium with a retractable roof. They draw plenty of raucous spectators.

Minute Maid Park   BASEBALL
(☑713-259-8000; 501 Crawford St) The Houston Astros (http://houston.astros.mlb.com) play pro baseball right downtown. The first retractable roof in town still attracts attention, or maybe it's the real steam train that chugs along after every home run. See the website for ballpark tour times.

 Shopping

For browsing in more eclectic and locally owned stores, hit the neighborhoods. Along 19th St (between Yale St and Shepherd Dr) in the Heights (www.houstonheights.org) you'll find unique antiques, clever crafts and cafes. On the first Saturday of every month, the street takes on a carnival-like air with outdoor booths and entertainment.

In Montrose Westheimer St is a dream for crafty fashionistas and antique-hunters alike. Start on Dunlavy Rd and work your way down the street, where you'll find a mix of used- and new-clothing stores running the gamut from vintage to punk rock to Tokyo mod, plus lots of funky old furniture.

For slightly less rebellious fashion terrain, stroll around Rice Village and let the window displays lure you in.

ℹ️ **Information**

Greater Houston Convention & Visitors Bureau
(☑713-437-5200; www.visithoustontexas.com; City Hall, 901 Bagby St; ☺9am-4pm Mon-Sat) As much a giant souvenir shop as an info center.
Houston Public Library (www.hpl.lib.tx.us; 500 McKinney St; ☺10am-6pm Mon, Tue & Thu, to 8pm Wed, to 5pm Sat; 📶) Free internet computers and wi-fi.

Main Post Office (401 Franklin St; ☺7am-7pm Mon-Fri, 8am-noon Sat) Plenty of parking, at the north edge of downtown.

Galveston

Don't think of Galveston as just another beach town. What makes it irresistible is that it's actually a historic town that happens to have some beaches. An easy day trip from Houston, it's also a very popular cruise-ship port, which has been a vital boost to the economy.

◉ **Sights & Activities**

Nothing more than a sandy barrier island, Galveston stretches 30 miles in length and is no more than 3 miles wide. The center of activity on the island, the historic 'Strand' district (around the intersection of 22nd and Mechanic Sts) is best covered on foot so you can check out the many attractions, shops, restaurants and bars. Find loads more dining and activity info at Galveston Island Visitors Center (☑409-797-5144; www.galveston.com; Ashton Villa, 2328 Broadway; ☺9am-5pm). For quick and easy beach access, park anywhere along the seawall. Or, if you want more sand to spread out on, head to East Beach (1923 Boddecker Dr, off Seawall Blvd; per vehicle $8; ☺dawn-dusk Mar-Oct) at the eastern end of the island.

Texas Seaport Museum
& Tallship Elissa   MUSEUM
See p42.

Moody Gardens   AMUSEMENT PARK
(www.moodygardens.com; 1 Hope Blvd; rainforest/aquarium/all-attraction day pass $22/22/60; ☺10am-6pm Sep-May, to 8pm Jun-Aug; 🚗) Three colorful glass pyramids form the focus of one entertainment complex. The Aquarium Pyramid showcases king penguins, fur seals and the largest array of sea horses in the world. The 10-story Rainforest Pyramid is a lush tropical jungle full of plants, birds, butterflies and a wonderful creepy-crawly bug exhibit. The Discovery Pyramid hosts traveling exhibits and some so-so space-related stuff.

 Sleeping & Eating

It's no surprise that the sea is the primary food source in Galveston; fish restaurants (mostly chains) line the bayside piers near the Strand.

Beachcomber Inn
MOTEL $

(☑409-744-7133; www.galvestoninn.com; 2825 61st St; r $80-130; P❄🏠🏊) A block removed from the beach, this basic two-story motel provides a neat-and-clean budget break. Minifridges and microwaves in every room.

★ Harbor House
BOUTIQUE HOTEL $$

(☑409-763-3321; www.harborhousepier21.com; Pier 21, off Harborside Dr; r $130-180; ❄🏠🏊) Stay among the shops and museums of the Pier 21 complex in the heart of the historic Strand district. Rustic touches accent the 42 large, comfy rooms occupying a re-created, wharfside warehouse. You have good views of the harbor through smallish windows.

★ Farley Girls
AMERICAN $

(801 Post Office St; mains $8-14; ⊘10:30am-9pm Mon-Fri, from 8:30am Sat & Sun) The historic building may be elegant, with fern-studded colonnades and high wood ceilings, but the tasty comfort food and counter service are down-home casual. Eclectic offerings include warm goat cheese and pecan salad, BBQ pulled pork and prosciutto pizza. At weekend brunch they serve tasty eggs Benedict, breakfast pizza, and eggs with their saucy Gouda-and-mushroom grits.

Oasis
VEGETARIAN $

(409 25th St; mains $5-10; ⊘10am-4pm Tue-Sat, 9am-2pm Sun; 🌱) An oasis in a deep-fried landscape, this inviting juice bar and cafe serves up delicious quinoa and beet salads,

vegetable panini, veggie burgers and other light bites. Breakfast (served till 2pm) is also good. It's near the historic Strand district.

Gaido's
SEAFOOD $$$

(☑409-762-9625; www.gaidos.com; 3800 Seawall Blvd; mains $20-35; ⊘noon-9pm) Run by the same family since 1911, Gaido's is easily the best-known and best-loved restaurant in Galveston. Expect vast platters of no-compromise seafood (oh, the oysters...) served on white tablecloths and with hushed tones. They have a more casual sister restaurant, Nick's Kitchen & Beach Bar http://nicksgalveston. com; mains $11-24; ⊘11am-10pm), next door.

🍷 Drinking & Nightlife

Galveston Island Brewing
MICROBREWERY

(☑409-740-7000; www.galvestonislandbrewing. com; 8423 Stewart Rd; ⊘4-10pm Mon-Thu, 3pm-midnight Fri, noon-midnight Sat, noon-10pm Sun) This local icon brews up some excellent quaffs, including a refreshing half-wheat, half-barley beer (the Tiki Wheat). There's a grassy yard where you can relax (while kids clamber about on the playground), watch the sunset (note the stadium seating) and mingle with a friendly Galveston crowd.

ℹ Getting There & Away

TO AND FROM THE AIRPORT
Houston Airport System (www.fly2houston.com) has two airports: **George Bush Intercontinental** (IAH) and **William P Hobby Airport** (HOU). Read your ticket closely: some airlines, such as Delta, fly out of both airports. You can find every major car-rental agency at either airport.

SuperShuttle (☑800-258-3826; www.super shuttle.com) provides regular services from both Bush ($25) and Hobby ($24) airports to hotels and addresses around town.

Cabs are readily available at both airports. Airport rates are determined by zone, and you'll pay either the flat zone rate or the meter rate, whatever's less. You'll shell out $50 to get from Bush to downtown; from Hobby it's about $25.

The **Metropolitan Transit Authority** (METRO; ☑713-635-4000; www.ridemetro.org; one-way $1.25) runs bus 102 between George Bush Intercontinental and downtown from 5:30am to 10:50pm. Bus 88 operates between Hobby and downtown 6am to 11pm every day except Sunday.

CAR & MOTORCYCLE
From Houston, follow I-45 southeast for 51 miles.

Hurricane Ike knocked the Galveston Island Trolley off the rails. Until it's restored – by 2017 at current estimates – you really need a car to get around.

Fox squirrel, Aransas National Wildlife Refuge
JEFF FOOTT / GETTY IMAGES ©

Aransas National Wildlife Refuge

For bird-watchers, the premier site on the Texas coast is the 115,000-acre Aransas National Wildlife Refuge (p43). The scenery alone is spectacular, and close to 400 bird species have been documented here. None are more famous than the extremely rare whooping cranes that summer in Canada and spend their winters in the refuge.

From the observation tower you can usually spot one or two, but boats tour the estuaries from November to March, and this is easily the best way to get a good view of the rare birds.

Rockport & Fulton

Coming from the north, leave TX 35 after you cross the LBJ Causeway and follow shoreline-hugging Fulton Beach Rd south first through Fulton and then into Rockport, where Austin St is the main drag of the walkable downtown. In either direction, avoid strip-mall-lined TX 35.

○ Sights & Activities

Rockport Harbor HARBOR
Crescent-shaped Rockport Harbor is one of the prettiest on the Gulf Coast. It's lined with all manner of boats (shrimp, fishing charter, tour and pleasure craft) and a series of rustic peel-and-eat shrimp joints and bait shops.

Texas Maritime Museum MUSEUM
(☑361-729-1271; www.texasmaritimemuseum.org; 1202 Navigation Circle, Rockport; adult/child $8/3; ☉10am-4pm Tue-Sat, 1-4pm Sun) Everything from fishing boats to offshore oil rigs to the story of the short-lived Texas Navy is covered at this large museum. Displays emphasize the human aspects of the Texas seacoast. Several old boats that were used to rescue people caught in storms are displayed outside.

Aquarium at Rockport Harbor AQUARIUM
(☑361-727-0016; www.rockportaquarium.com; 702 Navigation Circle; admission free; ☉1-4pm Thu-Mon) This small volunteer-run aquarium has crabs and other local sea critters, including most of the fish avidly sought by local fishers. You'll often see local artists just outside capturing the colors of the sea.

Rockport Center for the Arts CULTURAL CENTER
(☑361-729-5519; 902 Navigation Circle; ☉10am-4pm Tue-Sat,1-4pm Sun) It's worth popping in to this cheery center, housed partly in a charming 1890s building, to see what's going on with the lively local arts scene. It offers painting classes and is right on the water.

Fulton Mansion State Historical Park HISTORIC BUILDING
(☑361-729-0386; www.visitfultonmansion.com; 317 S Fulton Beach Rd; adult/child $6/4; ☉9:30am-4:30pm Tue-Sat, 12:30-4:30pm Sun) This imposing 1870s mansion comes as a surprise amid other more modern – and modest – shorefront buildings. It was built by George Fulton, who was clever with the design. On the outside, it looks like an imposing French Second Empire creation, right down to the mansard roofs.

Slowride KAYAKING
(☑361-758-0463; www.slowrideguide.com; 821 S Commercial, Aransas Pass; 4hr kayak rental $40) The estuaries of the coast are ideal for kayaking. You can rent kayaks at this shop just south of Rockport or arrange for guided fishing and ecotours.

🛏 Sleeping & Eating

The Fulton waterfront has a few modest motels near the mansion and there is another good patch down by Rockport Harbor.

Bayfront Cottages & Pier MOTEL, CABIN $
(☑361-729-6693; www.rockportbayfrontcottages.com; 309 S Fulton Beach Rd, Fulton; r $50-100; ❄🤖) A nicely updated old motor court is next to the mansion and across from the water. Use its pier to catch a fish, then cook it up in one of the small kitchens that come with each unit.

Hoope's House HISTORIC HOTEL $$
(☑361-729-8424; www.hoopeshouse.com; 417 N Broadway St, Rockport; r $110-175; ❄🤖🏊) This landmark mansion overlooks Rockport Harbor, and has four rooms in the main house and another four in a modern wing. It's plush without being fussy and there's a large pool and a fab breakfast on offer.

Apple Dumpling CAFE $
(☑361-727-2337; 118 N Magnolia St, Rockport; mains from $5; ☉8am-5pm Mon-Sat) Don't let the plain-Jane exterior deter you from this locally loved deli and cafe in downtown

Rockport. The homemade ice cream is creamy and dreamy and the sandwiches are just the thing for picnics amidst the local natural splendor.

Boiling Pot SEAFOOD $$
(☑361-729-6972; 2015 Fulton Beach Rd, Fulton; meals $18; ☺4-10pm Mon-Thu, 11am-11pm Fri & Sat, 11am-10pm Sun) This is a rustic classic, and a lot of fun. Mountains of shellfish plus potatoes, sausage and corn are put in a pot full of spicy boiling water; then dumped on your paper-covered table and you dive in (no cutlery, no crockery – bibs provided).

Latitude 2802 SEAFOOD $$$
(☑361-727-9009; www.latituderockport.com; 105 N Austin, Rockport; mains $15-33; ☺5-10pm Tue-Sun) The finest dining in the area. Look for creative takes on seafood at this stylish little place that includes an art gallery. The local special, grouper, is prepared several ways; sides vary seasonally. Shrimp and oyster dishes are also excellent.

❶ Information

Rockport-Fulton Area Chamber of Commerce (☑800-826-6441, 361-729-9952; www.rockport-fulton.org; 319 Broadway St, Rockport; ☺9am-5pm Mon-Fri, to 2pm Sat) This very helpful office is near Rockport Harbor.

Pelican, South Padre Island (p111)
DHUGHES9 / GETTY IMAGES ©

Port Aransas

Port A can be your base, or a stop on a looping drive around the bay.

◉ Sights

★ **Beaches** BEACH
Port A has 18 miles of silvery white beaches on the gulf side of Mustang Island. You can drive and park on the sand, though you may require a permit; the main access point is via Beach St (try to remember that) to the county-run **IB Magee Beach Park** (☑361-749-6117; www.nuecesbeachparks.com; Beach St).

Port Aransas Museum MUSEUM
(☑361-749-3800; www.portaransasmuseum.org; 101 E Brundrett St; ☺1-5pm Thu-Sat) **FREE** Volunteers make this small museum a delightful place to learn the history of Port A, from sand (when this was just a barrier island) to sea (when the residents were professional fishers) to sand and sea (when the economy was based on fishing and beachgoing for fun).

Nature Preserves NATURE RESERVE
(☑361-749-4158; Ross Ave & Port St; ☺dawn-dusk) **FREE** The city runs two birding centers that share views over the bird-filled marshes and salt flats on the east side of town. There are two points of access, and you can wander over 2 miles of boardwalks and partake in the feathery spectacle from observation decks and towers.

San José Island ISLAND
A privately owned island, known as St Jo to locals, is just across the ship channel from Port Aransas. This desert island is popular for fishing and beachcombing, although users are advised to bring over virtually everything they require, including water. The **jetty boat** (☑800-605-5448; www.jettyboat.net; 900 N Tarpon St; adult/child $12/6; ☺from 6.30am to 6pm) runs many times daily.

🏃 Activities

There are myriad places offering water adventures and gear for surfing, kiteboarding and more. Fishing is big business in Port A, and there are dozens of boats offering trips and private charters. The tourist bureau has listings. Rates vary widely, somewhere between $50 and $1000 or more, depending on whether you're going to the bay or gulf, the length of the trip and what exactly you're trying to catch. **Fisherman's Wharf** (☑800-605-5448; www.wharfcat.com; 900 N Tarpon St; 5hr trip adult/child $70/35) has regular deep-sea excursions and runs jetty boats to outer islands.

🛏 Sleeping

There are more motel/condo rooms in Port A than there are permanent residents, so there are plenty of options and something to meet most budgets. Not surprisingly, summer weekends are when rooms are at their dearest; book in advance. Lots of options give you easy access to the walkable part of Port A; avoid the unsightly large condo developments south of town.

★ **Amelia's Landing** MOTEL **$$**
(☑888-671-8088; www.ameliaslanding.com; 105 N Alister St; r $95-200; ❄🔊☃) This centrally located motel has an aviation theme, with each unit decorated for a different bit of flying lore (such as *Top Gun*, Apollo and the Wright Brothers). All are loaded with amenities (fridges, DVDs, microwaves) and some have kitchens. It books up early in high season.

Sea Breeze Suites HOTEL **$$**
(☑361-749-1500; www.seabreezeportaransas.com; 407 Beach St; r $120-220; ❄🔊☃) Close to both the beach and the center of town, the building won't win any architectural awards but the 24 rooms are large and have balconies with views of the gulf and channel. Each has a full kitchen.

★ **Tarpon Inn** HISTORIC HOTEL **$$**
(☑361-749-5555, 800-365-6784; www.thetarponinn.com; 200 E Cotter Ave; r $100-220; ❄🔊) Dating from 1900, this charming, rickety place has been rebuilt several times after hurricanes, most extensively after the 1919 big blow. The lobby has more than 7000 of the huge silver scales that come from tarpon, the 6ft-long namesake fish. Most of the 24 rooms are small and have no TVs or phones, but they do have lots of character and rocking chairs on the veranda.

🍴 Eating & Drinking

Port A has a great selection of restaurants and divey bars, almost all as casual as a bunch of sand in your shorts. Many have the kind of goofy vibe that helps make Port A the cool beach town that it is. Note that there're a lot of humdrum seafood places that fry up frozen fish: beware.

★ **Avery's Kitchen** CAFE **$$**
(☑361-749-0650; 200 W Ave G; mains from $10; ⊙7.30am-8pm Tue-Sat, to 2.30pm Sun & Mon) With

ℹ BEACH PARKING PERMITS

You can drive your vehicle right onto the sand at many points in Port Aransas and Mustang Island. In fact the beaches are usually so hard that even a regular car will have no problem – just look to see what others are doing. At city and county beaches, you'll need a beach parking permit ($12). These are easily purchased at convenience stores, supermarkets and at the Port A tourist office.

a large sunny deck, this cheap and cheerful cafe stays crowded by offering up excellent breakfasts, sandwiches and seafood specials.

Gaff BAR **$**
(☑361-749-5970; www.gotothegaff.com; 323 Beach St; mains from $9; ⊙11am-11pm Sun-Thu, to midnight Fri & Sat) Out by the beach, this shacky bar is perfect for one aspiring to arrested development. Fun includes belt sander races and chicken-poop bingo (come on bird, come on!). There's decent pizza and subs plus live music that includes blues and country. Most days are 'talk like a pirate day' here.

★ **Tarpon Ice House** BAR
See p45.

Shorty's BAR
(☑361-749-8224; www.shortysportaransas.com; 823 Tarpon St; mains from $7; ⊙10am-2am Mon-Sat, noon-2am Sun) The town's 'oldest and friendliest' watering hole is filled with local characters. It has dartboards and pool tables, and the ceiling is adorned with hundreds of caps from around the world. You can bar-hop around the block here, down by the docks.

Port Aransas Brewing BREWERY
(☑361-749-2739; 429 N Alister St; ⊙11am-8pm) The microbrews are darn tasty at this small bar and grill in the center (we like the Island Pale Ale) and they get points for also stocking bottles of some of the best microbrews from around the US. The burgers are thick, juicy and lauded (mains from $10). There's a small deck out front.

ℹ Information

Port Aransas Chamber of Commerce and Tourist Bureau (☑361-749-5919, 800-452-6278; www.portaransas.org; 403 W Cotter Ave; ⊙9am-5pm Mon-Fri, to 3pm Sat) Has stacks of brochures, maps and information. Loans out binoculars for bird-watching.

Padre Island National Seashore

The 60 southern miles of 'North' Padre Island that lie outside Corpus Christi city limits are all a protected part of the Padre Island National Seashore (p46). Four-wheel drive is necessary to see the extent of the park, but if you hike even a short distance from the visitor center, you'll be free of the crowds. The constant wind not only creates and moves dunes, it also attracts kitesurfers and windsurfers to the inland-side Bird Island Basin area.

True to its name, Horses on the Beach (☑361-949-4944; www.horsesonthebeachcorpus.com; SPID Park Rd 22; 1 hr group ride $40-45; 🐴) offers group horseback rides along the sands. Reserve ahead.

Camping is available at the park's semideveloped, paved Malaquite Campground (campsites $8). Or go primitive: beach camping is free with the Padre Island National Seashore entrance permit.

Watch for the endangered Kemp Ridley sea turtles that nest in the park and are closely protected. If you're visiting in late summer, you might be able to take part in a turtle release; call the Hatchling Hotline (☑361-949-7163) for information.

Corpus Christi

The salt breezes and palm-tree-lined bay are quite pleasant in this 'city by the sea', whose population numbers just over 300,000. Downtown has a waterfront promenade and a few museums, but there's not too much in town to entice visitors. Take a trip out to Padre Island National Seashore for a beachy break, though don't expect the windblown surf to be azure. To the north, Port Aransas is a bustling little fishing town with tons of restaurants and boat charters.

Shoreline Dr, in downtown Corpus, has a small beach; the street continues south as Ocean Dr, which has bayfront playgrounds and parks, as well as some serious mansions. Corpus Christi Convention & Visitors Bureau (☑800-678-6232; www.visitcorpuschristitx.org; 1590 N Shoreline Blvd; ⊙9am-5pm Mon-Thu, to 6pm Fri-Sun) has helpful coupons online.

◉ Sights

★USS Lexington Museum   MUSEUM
See p46.

Museum of Science & History   MUSEUM
(www.ccmuseum.com; 1900 N Chaparral St; adult/child $9/7; ⊙10am-5pm Tue-Sat, noon-5pm Sun & Mon; 🐴) Explore shipwrecks at this fun museum, right on the south side of the ship channel. See how Texas proved to be the French explorer La Salle's doom, and see the moldering remains of reproductions of two of Columbus' ships.

🛏 Sleeping & Eating

Bars and restaurants are clustered on the streets surrounding Chaparral and Water Sts downtown – there are few restaurants on the island.

Seashell Inn   MOTEL $
(☑361-888-5391; www.seashellinnmotel.com; 202 Kleberg Pl; r weekday/weekend $75/150; P✳🛜🏊) In North Beach the Seashell Inn has an unrivaled location overlooking the sandy shores. The remodeled rooms are in better shape than the aging facade, with comfy beds, a clean look and nice views.

V Boutique Hotel   BOUTIQUE HOTEL $$
(☑361-883-9200; www.vhotelcc.com; 701 N Water St; r $170-240, ste $320; P✳🛜) Adored by its guests, this small hotel in the heart of downtown offers a high level of service, and you can order room service from the excellent Vietnamese restaurant downstairs. It has eight comfy, well-equipped rooms, all with carpeting and a subdued modern design scheme; they range in size from studios to one-bedroom loft suites.

Cafe Hesters   CAFE $
(☑361-885-0151; www.hesterscafe.com; 1902 N Shoreline Blvd; mains $8-12; ⊙11am-3pm Tue-Fri, from 10am Sat) Nestled artfully in the Art Museum of South Texas, Hesters is much loved for its creative salads, delicious sandwiches and quiches, and beautiful desserts (key lime pie, brownies, raspberry cheesecake). It has a great outdoor setting overlooking the bridge. The original cafe (1714 S Alameda St; mains $7-10; ⊙7am-3pm Mon-Sat) in Six Points serves excellent breakfasts.

Executive Surf Club   SOUTHERN $
(309 N Water St; mains $6-10; ⊙11am-11pm Sun-Thu, to midnight Fri & Sat) Eat a fried-shrimp po'boy from a surfboard table and sip a craft brew from local Lazy Beach Brewing at this longtime fave. It has tables inside and out plus live music, and it's just divey enough for you to forget you're downtown.

Brewster Street

Icehouse   BURGERS, SEAFOOD **$$**

(1724 N Tancahua St; mains $8-16; ⊘11am-2am; 🖵) What feels like a big, open-sided roadhouse serves up good times via cold brews, live music (Thursday to Saturday nights), hearty pub grub and a huge deck. This place really rocks after baseball games at nearby Whataburger Field. Kids love the playground.

Harrison's Landing   SEAFOOD **$$**

(108 People's St, T-dock; mains $8-17; ⊘11am-9pm Sun-Thu, to 11pm Fri & Sat) Perched over the water, Harrison's Landing serves up blackened red snapper tacos, fish and chips, and juicy blue-cheese burgers in a casual, open-sided setting facing the marina. Those with sea legs can sit on the floating dock. There's live music Wednesday to Sunday nights.

Port Isabel

In the days before inexpensive hurricane insurance made South Padre Island (SPI) viable as a town, Port Isabel was the focus of life near the southern end of Texas. Records show that Spaniards and pirates both made frequent landfalls here in the 16th, 17th and 18th centuries.

Today Port Isabel is a must-stop just before SPI. Its small old town covers the waterfront for a couple of blocks on either side of the base of the TX 100 Queen Isabella Causeway. It is served by the free Wave shuttle to/from SPI.

◉ Sights

The three main sights are all close to each other and to the cute waterfront. You can buy combined tickets for all three (adult/child $9/4).

Port Isabel Lighthouse   HISTORIC BUILDING

See p46.

Port Isabel Historical Museum   MUSEUM

(☑956-943-7602; www.portisabelmuseums.com; 317 Railroad Ave; adult/child $4/2; ⊘10am-4pm Tue-Sat) Dating from 1899, and built sturdily of bricks to resist storms, the home of the history museum served at various times as the town's railroad station, post office and general store. You'll find it one block south of TX 100, near the lighthouse.

Treasures of the Gulf Museum   MUSEUM

See p46.

Eating

The waterfront is predictably lined with popular seafood joints and bars with decks overlooking the water. Go a few blocks inland for some of the best eats in the area.

Manuel's Restaurant   MEXICAN **$**

(☑956-943-1655; 313 Maxan St; mains from $6; ⊘7am-2pm Mon-Sat) That steady 'patting' sound you hear comes from the ladies in the back room making flour tortillas. Everything is dead-simple here, including the decor, but the classic Mexican fare is excellent. Get a side of avocado with anything you order, including the huevos rancheros at breakfast.

★ **Joe's Oyster Bar Restaurant**   SEAFOOD **$$**

(☑956-943-4501; 207 Maxan St; mains from $9; ⊘11am-7pm) Delight in seafood direct off the boats at this simple joint. They make a mean crab cake and the oysters are renowned. You can get anything to go for picnics or packed fresh for cooking later in the condo.

South Padre Island

South Padre Island has discovered gold in spring break, the period in March when hordes of college students congregate at beaches for a week or more of completely pleasurable excess that's limited only by the capacity of their livers, loins and billfolds. To welcome this annual bacchanal, this condo-crammed island has beach activities and bars galore.

The website of the South Padre Island Convention & Visitors Bureau (☑956-761-4412; www.spichamber.com; 610 Padre Blvd; ⊘9am-5pm) has a comprehensive list of mini-golf courses, restaurants, condo rentals and beachfront hotels. The Palms Resort (☑956-761-1316; www.palmsresortcafe.com; 3616 Gulf Blvd; r $120-230; 🛜🏊) is a friendly two-storey motel with a great seaside location (though rooms themselves don't have ocean views). The fun beachfront restaurant-bar serves some of the best food in South Padre.

Stop in for a drink or a meal at the Padre Island Brewing Company (☑956-761-9585; www.pibrewingcompany.com; 3400 Padre Blvd; mains from $10; ⊘11am-late), where you can wash down your burgers and seafood with a microbrew, or have a seafood feast at the ramshackle Pier 19 (1 Padre Blvd; mains $11-25; ⊘7am-11pm) jutting far over the water facing the bay (near the bridge).

Heart of Texas

Some of the area's purest pleasures are in its details: the scent of sage after rainfall, a flint quarry plied thousands of years ago, or the love songs written by young troubadours.

The vast open stretch of the Texas Panhandle and Plains is a region of long drives on lonely two-laners. Its cities are few and small. But it's not all tumbleweeds. Midland is at the heart of the Texas energy boom, Lubbock embodies the region's rich music heritage with its favorite son, Buddy Holly, and Amarillo keeps cattle king of the Panhandle. Natural wonders include America's second-largest canyon, Palo Duro, where the Comanche fought on long after other tribes gave in. But the region's greatest assets are the tiny towns seemingly lost in the past. Slumbering in the sun are forgotten architectural gems, and small-town cafes that have you itching for the next mealtime.

San Angelo

POP 93,200

⊙ Sights & Activities

★ **Fort Concho National Historic Landmark** HISTORIC SITE
See p52.

San Angelo Museum of Fine Arts MUSEUM
(SAMFA; ☑ 325-653-3333; www.samfa.org; 1 Love St; adult/child $2/1; ⊙ 10am-4pm Tue-Wed & Sat, to 6pm Thu, to 9pm Fri, 1-4pm Sun) This impressive saddle-shaped musuem is best known for its ceramics collection. Run in partnership with Angelo State University, SAMFA often has compelling special exhibits.

Concho Avenue Historic District HISTORIC SITE
See p52.

Miss Hattie's Bordello Museum MUSEUM
See p52.

Railway Museum of San Angelo MUSEUM
(☑ 325-486-2140; www.railwaymuseumsanangelo. homestead.com; 703 S Chadbourne St; adult/child $2/1; ⊙ 10am-4pm Sat) The beautifully renovated Santa Fe Depot is home to much railroad nostalgia. The station, on the El Paseo, is the main attraction. Inside the museum has models of 1920s San Angelo and old rail cars.

San Angelo State Park PARK
(☑ 325-949-4757; www.tpwd.state.tx.us; adult/child $4/free; ⊙ dawn-dusk) This state park is on the western outskirts of town, accessible via FM 2288 (Loop 2288) off W Ave N (which becomes Arden Rd west of downtown), US 87 or US 67. The 7600-acre park surrounds the 1950s reservoir, OC Fisher Lake. More than 50 miles of trails mean the parks are popular with animal- and bird-watchers.

Producer's Livestock Auction SPECTACLE
(☑ 325-653-3371; www.producersandcargile.com; 1131 N Bell St; ⊙ 9am Tue & Thu) **FREE** No one has a baaad time at the largest sheep auc-

tion in the USA, the Producer's Livestock Auction. Sheep are sold on Tuesday and cattle on Thursday. The auctioneers' banter is the most fascinating aspect of the whole deal – it's totally incomprehensible.

El Paseo de Santa Angela   WALKING TOUR
The El Paseo is a family-friendly, pleasure-filled stroll that is part of the 4-mile-long river walk that follows the Concho, from just west of downtown heading east to Bell St. Celebration Bridge links San Angelo's main street, Concho Ave, to the main attractions south of the river, which include a collection of historic buildings along Orient St.

⚔ Festivals & Events

The annual San Angelo Stock Show & Rodeo Cowboys Association Rodeo (www.san angelorodeo.com) runs over two weeks in February. It is one of the largest in the Southwest.

🛏 Sleeping

Most motels are situated on the major highways on the edge of town. Check with the tourist office for a list of the many good B&Bs.

Inn of the Conchos   MOTEL $
(☑325-658-2811, 800-621-6041; www.inn-of-the-conchos.com; 2021 N Bryant Blvd; r $50-100; ❄ 🛜 ⊠) On the northwest edge of downtown US 87, this is an older, modest 125-room motel that is valiantly hanging on in the face of the chains. Free hot breakfast buffet plus microwaves and fridges in the rooms are its ammo.

★ Sealy Flats Blues Inn   INN $$
(☑325-653-0437; www.sealyflats.com; 204 S Oakes St; r $120-200; ❄ 🛜) Part of the excellent downtown blues club and diner, this inn is housed in a much-restored historic hotel.

Inn at the Art Center   B&B $$
(☑325-658-3333; www.innattheartcenter.com; 2503 Martin Luther King; r $85-135; ❄ 🛜) Funky is an understatement for this three-room B&B at the back of the bohemian Chicken Farm Art Center. Rooms are as artful as you'd expect at a 1970s chicken farm turned artists' co-op.

🍴 Eating & Drinking

San Angelo has several excellent pubs right downtown.

Charcoal House   BURGERS $
(☑325-657-2931; 1205 N Chadbourne St; mains from $4; ⊙7am-9pm) The name raises great hopes for the burgers, and they deliver. Options abound at this traditional drive-in with in-car (or truck) service. Details such as the thick bacon win raves, as do the breakfasts.

Packsaddle Bar-B-Que   BARBECUE $
(☑325-949-0616; 6007 Knickerbocker Rd; mains $6-8; ⊙11am-8pm Wed-Mon) Don't let the downmarket location in a strip mall 6 miles southwest of the center put you off – the brisket here is among the finest you'll find anywhere in these parts (and beyond). It's bone-simple here, but it has diverting Nascar displays.

★ Peasant Village Restaurant   DELI/BISTRO $$
(☑325-655-4811; 23 S Park St; lunch mains from $8, dinner mains $17-27; ⊙11am-1:30pm Mon, 11am-1:30pm & 5-9pm Tue-Fri, 5-9pm Sat) Located in a beautiful 1920s house near downtown, creative mains of steak and seafood plus seasonal specials highlight the menu. Enjoy the best deli sandwiches, salads and desserts in town at lunch.

Miss Hattie's Café & Saloon   SOUTHERN $$
(☑325-653-0570; 26 E Concho Ave; mains from $8; ⊙11am-8pm Mon-Sat, but hours can vary) This place tips its hat to the bordello museum up the block, with early-20th-century decor featuring tapestries and gilt-edged picture frames. However, the tasty meat is the main attraction, especially the hunk of seasoned beef grilled into a hamburger and finished with an array of yummy toppings.

Sealy Flats   MUSIC BAR
(☑325-653-1400; www.sealyflats.com; 208 S Oakes St; ⊙11am-late) A real find if you want to hear live blues. There's open-mike night on Monday, local acts the rest of the week and usually well-known blues musicians on weekends. The back terrace is where it's at. Get a brew and enjoy the jammin'.

🛍 Shopping

San Angelo is well known for the pearls that form in the Concho River. These precious orbs occur naturally – and they're not just any pearls. They come in shades of pink and purple, usually in pastels but occasionally in vivid shades.

Historic Concho Ave has antique shops and vintage-clothing stores.

Wildflowers, Palo Duro Canyon State Park (p119)
HOLGER LEUE / GETTY IMAES ©

Eggemeyer's General Store   GIFTS
(☑ 325-655-1166; 35 E Concho Ave) This old-style place has penny candy and lots of gift-item nonsense. (OK we like the fudge.)

Legend Jewelers   JEWELRY
(☑ 325-653-0112; 18 E Concho Ave; ⊙ 10am-5pm Mon-Sat) The best place to shop for Concho River pearls.

JL Mercer & Son   WESTERN WEAR
(☑ 325-658-7634; www.jlmercerboots.com; 224 S Chadbourne St; ⊙ 10am-5pm Mon-Sat) Noted for its custom boots, spurs and other Western gear. Texas legends such as Lyndon Johnson got their boots here (as did on-screen cowboy John Wayne). Custom boots start at $600, but with options (there are many!) you can scoot past $2000 without breaking stride.

Chicken Farm Art Center   ARTS & CRAFTS
(☑ 325-653-4936;   www.chickenfarmartcenter. com; 2502 Martin Luther King Blvd; ⊙ 10am-5pm Tue-Sat) More than 20 artists create and display their works in studios in this old chicken farm. Many also live here.

ℹ Information

Helpful **San Angelo Convention and Visitors Bureau** (☑ 325-655-4136, 800-375-1206; www.visitsanangelo.org; 418 W Ave B; ⊙ 9am-5pm Mon-Sat, noon-4pm Sun) has a stunning location on the Concho River, near

downtown. A pedestrian bridge links to a groovy kids' playground.

ℹ Getting There & Around

Located just a bit west of Texas' geographic center, San Angelo is at the intersection of US 67, US 87 and US 277. Within town, US 87 becomes Bryant Blvd, which – along with Chadbourne St – is the city's main north–south road.

Around San Angelo

◎ Sights & Activities

**Fort McKavett State
Historical Park**   HISTORIC SITE
See p50.

Presidio de San Sabá   HISTORIC SITE
(www.presidiodesansaba.com;   off   US   190; ⊙ 8am-5pm) FREE What was once the largest Spanish fort in Texas has been beautifully restored. Presidio de San Sabá dates to 1757 and is close to the town of Menard, some 21 miles northeast of Fort McKavett. The site is great for wandering, especially when it's just you, bird calls and the buzz of cicadas.

X Bar Ranch   RANCH
(☑ 888-853-2688, 325-853-2688; www.xbarranch. com; 5 N Divide, Eldorado; day use $10) Near Eldorado, a town best known for its wool mills, this 7100-acre ranch may be just what you're looking for if you're hankering for a real Western holiday. There's horseback riding, of course, plus stargazing, hikes to view Indian mounds, bird-watching and ranch activities. Accommodation at the ranch includes campsites (from $10) and comfortable cabins (from $100). The ranch is 40 miles south of San Angelo, off US 277.

Laredo
POP 252,309

Laredo makes for a good stop on any Rio Grande itinerary. Its historic old downtown is evocative and there are some enticing dining options for Mexican-food fans.

🛏 Sleeping & Eating

La Posada Hotel & Suites   HISTORIC HOTEL $$
(☑ 956-722-1701; www.laposada.com; 1000 Zaragoza St, San Agustín Plaza; r $110-200; ❄ @ 🛜 🐕 🏊) This hacienda-style hotel occupies a downtown complex of buildings dating from 1916. The stylish rooms surround two large pools and gardens.

El Meson De San Agustin
MEXICAN $
(www.elmesondesanagustin.com; 908 Grant St; mains from $6; ⊙11am-4:30pm Mon-Sat) Superb food issues forth at this tiny little, uber-non-descript family-run restaurant. Seemingly humdrum fare like enchiladas and chips and salsa reach heights few thought possible.

Palenque Grill
MEXICAN $$
(☏956-728-1272; www.palenquegrill.com; 7220 Bob Bullock Loop; mains $10-18; ⊙11am-11pm) The upscale menu is ambitious and features regional cuisine from around Mexico.

Big Spring
POP 27,300

The relentlessly flat Permian Basin landscape starts to show signs of a change 40 miles east of Midland. Big Spring is on the edge of the Edwards Plateau Caprock Escarpment, the defining topographical feature of the Texas Panhandle. The spring for which the town is named sits in Comanche Trail Park.

Nearby, the nature trail at Big Spring State Park (p52) has labels describing the hearty plants, such as the spiky argarita bush. A short drive around the top of the park has sweeping views across the basin and plateau.

The 15-story Hotel Settles (☏432-267-7500; www.hotelsettles.com; 200 E Third St; r $150-300; ❉⊛⊠) tells a classic Texas story: born during a 1930s boom, it eventually closed, leaving a humungous corpse looming over an otherwise tiny town. Enter G Brint Ryan, a local boy who made zillions helping corporations avoid taxes. He bought the Settles' remains and millions of dollars later it reopened in 2013 as a lavish hotel.

The Settles definitely looms large locally and although public areas have been restored to period glory, the suites and smaller guest rooms are modern and lavish. There's a top-end restaurant and a sumptuous bar, perfect for sipping bourbon and telling lies.

Lubbock
POP 229,500

'Lubbock or leave it' sing the Dixie Chicks, but this seemingly characteristic bit of Texas bravado isn't what it seems, as the song includes sardonic lines such as 'Got more churches than trees.' And while you'll see plenty of steeples on the horizon, what will really strike you about west Texas' liveliest city is its celebration of life beyond cotton and cows.

Buddy Holly grew up in Lubbock and the town celebrates his legacy in both attractions and an entire entertainment district. The other big sound happens on fall weekends when the roar of fans at sport-mad Texas Tech's football games can stop a tumbleweed in its tracks.

Lubbock is known as 'Hub City' because so many major highways meet here.

⊙ Sights

Buddy Holly's roots in Lubbock are reason enough to visit.

★Buddy Holly Center
MUSEUM
(☏806-767-2686; www.buddyhollycenter.org; 1801 Crickets Ave; adult/child $5/2; ⊙10am-5pm Tue-Sat, from 1pm Sun) A huge version of Holly's trademark horn-rims mark the Buddy Holly Center. The center is home to the Buddy Holly Gallery; a room devoted to the man with those glasses and pristine teeth. The gallery includes some of his schoolbooks, shoes and records, but best of all are Holly's Fender Stratocaster and hallmark glasses.

Buddy Holly Statue
& Walk of Fame
MONUMENT
(8th St at Ave Q) In front of the Civic Center, a larger-than-life-size statue of Holly is surrounded by plaques honoring him and other west Texans who made it big in arts and entertainment.

Buddy Holly's Grave
CEMETERY
(2011 E 31st St, east of Martin Luther King Jr Blvd; ⊙dawn-dusk) The headstone in the Lubbock City Cemetery reads 'In Loving Memory of Our Own Buddy Holley. September 7, 1936 to February 3, 1959.' Some visitors leave guitar picks, coins and other tokens. The cemetery is located on the eastern edge of town. Once inside the gate, turn down the lane to your right.

★National Ranching
Heritage Center
MUSEUM
(☏806-742-0498; www.nrhc.ttu.edu; 3121 4th St; ⊙10am-5pm Mon-Sat, 1-5pm Sun) FREE A real Lubbock gem, this open-air museum, part of the Texas Tech museum complex, tells a detailed story of what life was like on the Texas High Plains from the late 1700s until the Dust Bowl era of the 1930s. Nearly 50 preserved ranch structures are arrayed on 16 acres.

Lubbock Lake Landmark HISTORIC SITE
(☑806-742-1116; www.museum.ttu.edu/lll; 2401 Landmark Dr; ⊘9am-5pm Tue-Sat, 1-5pm Sun) FREE Another Tech-run attraction, this site is a sort of time capsule for all the cultures that have inhabited the South Plains for the last 12,000 years. Bones of critters such as woolly mammoths were first unearthed here when agricultural irrigation caused Lubbock Lake's water table to decline in the 1930s, and excavations have gone on here since 1939.

To get here, follow Loop 289 to Clovis Rd west of I-27 on the northwest side of town.

Mackenzie Park PARK
(at US 87 & 4th St; ⊘dawn-dusk) Located off I-27 at Broadway St and Ave A, 248-acre Mackenzie Park has two dynamite highlights amid what's otherwise a mundane urban park.

Prairie dogs are the stars of **Prairie Dog Town**, a hugely popular 7-acre habitat for the winsome rodents who keep busy excavating their 'town' and watching for groundskeepers.

The irresistibly named **Joyland** (☑806-763-2719; www.joylandpark.com; admission $6-19; ⊘varies mid-Mar–Oct, until 10pm Jun-Aug) has three roller coasters, 30 other rides and an array of carnival arcades and games that are little changed from Holly's time.

American Wind Power Center MUSEUM
(☑806-747-8734; www.windmill.com; 1701 Canyon Lake Dr; admission $5; ⊘10am-5pm Tue-Sat year-round, 2-5pm Sun summer) A squeaky windmill is part of the iconic opening to *Once Upon a Time in the West,* and you can see more than 90 examples of these Western icons at the American Wind Power Center, located on a 28-acre site at E Broadway St south of Mackenzie Park. Seen together, the windmills form their own compelling sculpture garden.

★ Festivals & Events

National Cowboy Symposium and Celebration FESTIVAL
(☑806-798-7825; www.cowboy.org) September is a big time in Lubbock, with returning Tech students and this huge gathering of cowboys, cowboy wannabes, cowboy scholars, cowboy musicians and cowboy cooks. Yee-haw!

🛏 Sleeping

There are several motels on Ave Q just south of US 82. They are close to downtown and a reasonable 1.3-mile walk southeast to the Depot District. There's another cluster of chains south of the center at exit 1 off I-27, and still more scattered along TX 289, the ring road southwest of town.

Buffalo Springs Lake CAMPGROUND $
(☑806-747-3353; www.buffalospringslake.net; FM 835 & E 50th St; tent sites $15-35; ☎ ☀ ☀) The lake is 5 miles southeast of Lubbock and is big on fun (think ATV trails) as opposed to natural splendor. Sites vary from basic tent-only ones to those with full hookups.

Koko Inn MOTEL $
(☑800-782-3254, 806-747-2591; 5201 Ave Q; r $50-100; ❄ ☎ ☀ ☀) This locally owned non-chain motel has character. You can lounge around on the large redwood deck that surrounds the indoor pool – perfect during a winter blast. Rooms have fridges and microwaves. There's a lively nightclub; this south-side neighborhood is a bit frayed.

Woodrow House B&B $$
(☑806-793-3330; www.woodrowhouse.com; 2629 19th St; r $100-180; ❄ ☎) Right across from Texas Tech, this professionally run B&B offers a range of themed rooms. Up-and-comers may enjoy the sumptious charms of the Honeymoon Suite, while those who prefer to bring up the rear may enjoy the suite in an actual caboose in the garden.

Overton Hotel HOTEL $$$
(☑806-776-7000; www.overtonhotel.com; 2322 Mac Davis Lane; r $120-350; ❄ @ ☎) The best place to stay in town, the 15-story independently owned Overton is close to the Tech campus. From the valets to the turn-down service this is a luxurious hotel. Percolate your cares away in the Jacuzzi then unwind in your boldly decorated room.

✕ Eating

Good restaurants are scattered around town, although you won't go wrong basing yourself in the Depot District and browsing. An organic **farmers market** (cnr Ave A & 19th St; ⊘9am-5:30pm Mon-Sat Jun-Nov) sells the best produce from the region.

Ranch House Restaurant AMERICAN $
(☑806-762-3472; 1520 Buddy Holly Ave; mains from $5; ⊘6am-4pm Mon-Sat) Formica tables and waiters who know what you want before your mouth can form the words help make this huge old diner a classic. Eggs fuel the breakfast hordes, while lunchers vie for pot roast and Red Top stew (beef, carrots and chilies).

Tom & Bingos Bar-B-Que BARBECUE $
(☑806-799-1514; 3006 34th St; mains from $6; ⊘10:30am-4pm Mon-Sat) This shack is a bit scruffy, but appearances are forgotten when you taste the smoked ham and brisket sand-

wiches (have the latter chopped). Sides are few: use the fries to mop up the tangy, sweet sauce. Open since 1952.

★ Crafthouse Gastropub
BISTRO $$

(📞806-687-1466; www.crafthousepub.com; 3131 34th St; mains $9-22; ⏰11am-10pm Mon-Thu, 11am-midnight Fri & Sat; 🖌) Lubbock's most creative restaurant is the work of Jason and Kate Diehl. From the pickled seasonal vegetables on the starter list to inventive seasonal fare, it has something to catch your eye. Mindful of local budgets, it serves cheeseburgers, but what burgers they are. The twice-fried fries are sublime. The beer and wine list is superb.

★ La Diosa Cellars
TAPAS $$

(📞806-744-3600; 901 17th St; mains $5-20; ⏰11am-10pm Tue-Thu, to midnight Fri & Sat) One of several local wineries, La Diosa uncorks a range of Texas wines that goes beyond its own label. There's inventive Mediterranean-style snacks and meals as well as a coffee bar. On many nights there's live entertainment. Come for a glass of wine, a snack, a meal or just to get down. A Depot District fave.

Triple J Chop House
& Brewery
STEAKHOUSE $$

(📞806-771-6555; 1807 Buddy Holly Ave; mains from $12; ⏰11am-10pm Mon-Thu, to midnight Fri & Sat) The airy, exposed-brick dining room has a glass wall looking into a microbrewery. The White Gold Cream and Sip-O-Whit are in a class of their own. Steaks live up to west Texas standards and there are tasty alternatives with a Southwestern flair.

🍸 Drinking & Nightlife

Go!, a free weekly by the town's wonderfully named newspaper, the *Lubbock Avalanche-Journal*, has full listings of what's on.

The Depot District is Lubbock's nightlife HQ, and covers a few blocks adjoining Buddy Holly Ave between 17th and 19th Sts. Otherwise, raucous bars, cheap burrito joints and plasma-TV dealers mark the classic college neighborhood where Broadway crosses University Ave into the campus.

★ Blue Light
LIVE MUSIC

(📞806-762-3688; www.thebluelightlive.com; 1806 Buddy Holly Ave; ⏰noon-late) This legendary club has plenty of live Texas country and rock. Watch for hall-of-famer Gary P Nunn.

Cactus Courtyard
BAR

(📞806-535-5610; www.cactuscourtyard.com; 1801 Buddy Holly Ave; ⏰3pm-late Apr-Oct) Huge

open-air venue with west Texas music and all the domestic beers you can quaff.

☆ Entertainment

Cactus Theater
THEATER

(📞806-747-7047; www.cactustheater.com; 1812 Buddy Holly Ave) This handsome 1938 theater mostly presents variety shows, including the *Buddy Holly Story, Always...Patsy Cline* and *Honky Tonk Angels*.

Texas Tech Sports
SPECTATOR SPORTS

(www.texastech.com/tickets) For alumni and most locals, Texas Tech's sports teams, the Red Raiders, are a huge deal. Both the football team and the men's basketball team had great success in the last decade.

🛍 Shopping

Dollar Western Wear
WESTERN WEAR

(📞806-793-2818; 5011 Slide Rd; ⏰10am-6pm Mon-Sat) This place is among the biggest of Lubbock's many Western-gear shops.

ℹ Information

Buddy Holly had a live show on KDAV AM 1590 in the 1950s. It still plays music from the era and streams from www.kdav.org/kdav. **Visit Lubbock** (📞800-692-4035, 806-747-5232; www.visitlubbock.org; 1500 Broadway St, 6th fl; ⏰9am-5pm Mon-Fri) has a small selection of brochures.

Around Lubbock

Down in the Texas Hill Country, wine seems to make sense. Up here on the boot-scootin,' teetotalin' High Plains, it sounds like a joke. But hold those 'yucks,' as the Lubbock region has near-ideal wine-grape-growing conditions: sandy soil, hot days and cool nights.

Cabernets are the local specialty and more than 20 vineyards are now producing bold reds. You can try many of these while in Lubbock at La Diosa Cellars, a welcoming wine bar run by its namesake winery. Several others are good for a visit, and tours are generally free.

◉ Sights & Activities

Llano Estacado Winery
WINERY

(📞806-863-2704; www.llanowine.com; 3426 E FM 1585, east of US 87; ⏰10am-5pm Mon-Sat, noon-5pm Sun) Llano's (pronounced yah-no's) was founded in 1976, making it not only the largest but also the oldest of the modern Texas wineries. Among the two dozen wines produced, the Chardonnays have won plaudits.

CapRock Winery
WINERY

(📞 806-686-4452; www.caprockwinery.com; 408 E Woodrow Rd, south of FM 1585, half a mile east of US 87; ⊙ 10am-5pm Mon-Sat, 12:30-5pm Sun) About 4 miles southwest of Llano Estacado, Cap-Rock Winery is worth a visit for its beautiful Mission-style headquarters. CapRock makes about a dozen wines.

Pheasant Ridge Winery
WINERY

(📞 806-746-6033; www.pheasantridgewinery.com; 3507 E County Rd 5700; ⊙ noon-6pm Fri & Sat, 1-5pm Sun) Located 14 miles north of Lubbock near the town of New Deal, this winery is known for its range of wines, including the expected cabs but also a zesty chenin blanc.

Apple Country
Hi-Plains Orchards
OUTDOORS

(📞 806-892-2961; www.applecountryorchards.com; 12206 E US 62/82; ⊙ 9am-6pm Mon-Sat, to 4pm Sun) In spring, the sweet smell of apple blossoms perfumes the air as you head east of Lubbock on US 62/82. Some 16 miles east of the city is this spot with pick-your-own apple orchards, a popular lunch cafe and a shop that sells produce, including wild honey.

Along Texas Hwy 70

Evocative small towns – some thriving, others nearly gone – are found throughout west Texas. One little burg after another seems ripped from the pages of a Larry McMurtry novel. Texas Hwy 70 manages to link a string of these nearly forgotten places: a drive along this road takes you further from the 21st century than the mere miles traveled.

Begin in the south in Sweetwater, along I-20, some 40 miles west of Abilene. Long and lonely vistas of lush ranch land await as you drive north on Hwy 70. About 55 miles north, turn west at the T-junction with US 380 and drive 5 miles to the nearly evaporated ghost town of Claremont. About all that remains is a red stone jail, which could be a movie set.

Return east and rejoin Hwy 70. Some 40 miles of occasional rivers, scattered annuities (oil wells) and countless cattle later, you're in the modestly named hamlet of Spur. Most of the once-proud brick structures downtown are barely hanging on, like a chimney with bad grout. Stop into Dixie Dog Drive-In (216 W Hill St; mains from $3; ⊙ 8am-8pm) for a timeless small-town fast-food experience.

Just another 11 miles north brings you to the seat of Dickens County: Dickens. Anoth-

er fading burg, here you can still sense the pride of the original settlers in the massive courthouse built from carved limestone. Catch up on all the gossip at TC's Ponderosa (📞 806-623-5260; 136 US 82; mains from $5; ⊙ 7am-8pm), which is inside a gas station. Great barbecue is served up simply on Formica tables. Try the hot links, and get a pickled egg and a pineapple pudding for the road.

From here it is nearly 57 miles almost due north through verdant cattle and cotton country to Turkey. Pause in towns such as Roaring Springs in Motley County for smatterings of tiny shops that will never attract the attention of Wal-Mart.

Turkey
POP 380

The lovely lady in city hall told us that 'people are dying too quick.' And indeed, Turkey has been shrinking for decades. But amid the grizzled streets is a not-to-be-missed cultural attraction, the Bob Wills Museum (p53).

Turkey celebrates Wills' legacy with Bob Wills Days (www.bobwillsday.com; ⊙ late April), when 10,000 or more people stuff themselves into Turkey for a weekend of pickin' and grinnin', with jam sessions galore.

Palo Duro Canyon

The pancake-flat Texas plains have some real texture at Palo Duro Canyon, it's just that all the drama is below the horizon rather than above it. The meandering gorge is a place of brilliant colors and vibrant life (the name means 'hard wood', for the groves of mesquite). The nearby town of Canyon, 20 miles south of Amarillo, makes for a comfy base.

Canyon
POP 13,600

Besides being home to an excellent history museum, the Panhandle-Plains Historical Museum, Canyon is an ideal starting spot for Palo Duro Canyon State Park.

◉ Sights

★ Panhandle-Plains
Historical Museum
MUSEUM

See p54.

🛌 Sleeping

The drive south from Amarillo can be a chore at busy times, so it's better to stay in Canyon for a visit to the park. Campers should head straight to the park.

Buffalo Inn
MOTEL $

(📞 806-655-2124, 800-526-9968; www.buffaloinn canyontx.com; 300 23rd St/US 87; r $40-75; ❋ 🐾) This classic 1950s single-story motor court is centrally located by the west Texas A&M campus. It's snappily maintained and has the charm lacking in new chains.

Best Western Palo Duro Canyon
MOTEL $$

(📞 806-655-1132; www.bestwestern.com; 2801 4th Ave; r $70-180; ❋ @ 🐾 ❋ 🐾) As tidy inside as the white paint is outside, this recently built 51-unit motel lacks any regional charm but is convenient to the canyon and I-27. The pool, alas, is indoors, away from the balmy Texas air.

Eating

Canyon has good eats, but choices in the canyon itself are basic.

Ranch House Cafe
AMERICAN $

(📞 806-655-8785; 810 23rd St; mains from $6; ⊙ 7am-9pm) Look for the classic trapezoidal red sign along the old US 87 strip. Chicken-fried steak and chicken-fried chicken (!) lead the long list of diner specials. Ponder the posies on the spare yellow exterior and then enter a kingdom of fresh north Texas chow.

Feldman's Wrong Way Diner
AMERICAN $

(📞 806-655-2700; www.feldmansdiner.com; 1701 5th Ave; mains from $7; ⊙ 11am-9pm; ❢) As the menu says, this classy diner is dedicated to anyone who has made a wrong turn, wrong decision or wandered off the beaten path. Here, at least, you'll know you've done the right thing. Steaks, chicken and burgers star and are supported by a cast of sides including perfect okra and lovely broccoli. Lots of salads too. Look for the wind sock on the roof.

Palo Duro Canyon State Park

Attracting hikers, horseback riders and mountain bikers eager for recreation, Palo Duro Canyon State Park (p54) also draws artists and photographers for its magnificent blend of color and desert light.

The best time to visit is in the fall or winter because it gets dang hot here in the summertime (carry lots of water!)

🏃 Activities

There are plenty of great mountain-biking trails throughout the canyon, but nowhere to rent bikes.

SCENIC DRIVE: TEXAS 207 HIGHWAY

Many Panhandle locals say the best views of Palo Duro Canyon aren't in the park, are along TX 207 between Claude and Silverton in the south. This quiet 48-mile stretch enters the canyon lands about 13 miles south of Claude (where the 1963 Paul Newman classic *Hud* was filmed). Some of the most dramatic scenery is at the crossings of the Prairie Dog Town Fork with the Red River and Tule Creek. From Silverton both Turkey and Caprock Canyons are short drives.

Old West Stables
HORSEBACK RIDING

(📞 806-488-2180; www.oldweststables.com; 11450 Park Road 5; rides from $35; ⊙ Mar-Nov) Offers a variety of trips in Palo Duro Canyon.

Lighthouse Trail
HIKING

Palo Duro's most popular hiking trail leads to the Lighthouse, a hoodoo-style formation that's nearly 300ft tall. Almost all of the nearly 6-mile round-trip is flat and easily traversed. The floodplain to the southwest of the trail has perhaps the park's greatest concentration of wildlife, including aoudad sheep, white-tailed mule deer and wild turkeys.

🛏 Sleeping & Eating

For motels and restaurants, you'll need to be in Canyon or Amarillo. The park's campsites (sites $12-24) range from attractive and remote, and aimed at backpackers, to regular sites with full hookups. Cabins (📞 512-389-8900; per night $60-125) are a treat but there are only seven, so reserve ahead.

For supplies and burgers, try the Trading Post (📞 806-488-2821; www.paloduro tradingpost.us; 11450 Park Road 5; mains from $7; ⊙ 8:30am-7:30pm Mon-Sat, 11am-7pm Sun Mar-Nov).

ℹ Information

A small but pretty 1934 visitors center overlooks the canyon, and has interpretive exhibits on the area's geology and history, the region's best bookstore and good tourist info.

ℹ Getting There & Away

The park is at the end of TX 217, 12 miles east of Canyon and 24 miles southeast of Amarillo.

Amarillo

POP 193,700

Long an unavoidable stop, roughly halfway between Chicago and LA on old Route 66, Amarillo continues to figure in travel plans, simply by being the brightest light on the 543-mile stretch of I-40 between Oklahoma City, OK, and Albuquerque, NM.

⊙ Sights

Cadillac Ranch   MONUMENT

(I-40, btwn exits 60 & 62) To millions of people whizzing across the Texas Panhandle each year, the Cadillac Ranch, also known as Amarillo's 'Bumper Crop,' is the ultimate symbol of the US love affair with wheels. A salute to Route 66 and the spirit of the American road, it was created by burying, hood first, 10 west-facing Cadillacs in a wheat field outside town. The cars are easily spotted off the access road on the south side of I-40. The accepted practice today is to leave your own mark on the art by drawing on the disintegrating cars, which gives them an ever-changing patina. Bring spray paint in case other visitors haven't left any around.

Wonderland
Amusement Park   AMUSEMENT PARK

(☑806-383-3344; www.wonderlandpark.com; 2601 Dumas Dr, off US 87 north of the centre; admission $14-25; ☺Apr-Aug; ♿) If plowing along sedately for hours on the bland interstate has you ready for a little more excitement, then careening through the double loops of this park's Texas Tornado roller coaster should shake you out of your lethargy. A fun local amusement park, Wonderland has thrill rides, family rides and a water park. Check the online calendar for opening days and hours.

★ Amarillo Livestock Auction   SPECTACLE

(☑806-373-7464; www.amarillolivestockauction.com; 100 S Manhattan St; ☺10am Mon) A slice of the real West is on display every Tuesday morning at the Amarillo Livestock Auction, just north of SE 3rd Ave on the city's east side. The auction is still one of the state's largest, moving more than 100,000 animals annually (down from its 1970s peak of 715,000).

★ American Quarter Horse
Hall of Fame & Museum   MUSEUM

(☑806-376-5181; www.aqha.com; 2601 I-40 E exit 72A; adult/child $6/2; ☺9am-5pm Mon-Sat) Quarter horses, favored on the Texas range,

were originally named for their prowess at galloping down early American racetracks, which were a quarter-mile long. These beautiful animals are celebrated at this visually striking museum, which fully explores their roles in ranching and racing.

Don Harrington Discovery Center   MUSEUM

(☑806-355-9547; www.dhdc.org; 1200 Streit Dr; adult/child $10/7; ☺9:30am-4:30pm Tue-Sat, from noon Sun; ♿) Sadly you can't inhale any helium and talk like Donald Duck, but the lighter-than-air gas that was an Amarillo industry is honored at the Don Harrington Discovery Center. Aquariums, a planetarium and science exhibits (including a good one on birds of prey) round out a visit.

Wildcat Bluff Nature Center   NATURE RESERVE

(☑806-352-6007; www.wildcatbluff.org; 2301 N Soncy Rd; adult/child $7/2; ☺dawn-dusk) Stretch those road legs at this 600-acre nature center, which has trails winding through grasslands, cottonwoods and bluffs. Spy on a prairie-dog town and try to spot a burrowing owl or porcupine while avoiding rattlesnakes and tarantulas. The center is just northwest of town, off TX 335.

⁂ Festivals & Events

Coors Cowboy Club Ranch Rodeo   RODEO

(☑806-378-3096; www.coorsranchrodeo.com; ☺early Jun) Huge rodeo and ranch trade show.

World Championship Ranch Rodeo   RODEO

(☑806-374-9722; www.wrca.org; ☺early Nov) Real-deal cowboy world-championship.

🛏 Sleeping

With the notable exception of the Big Texan Inn, most of Amarillo's motel accommodations are chains (in fact there can't be one brand missing from the endless slew along I-40. Exits 64, 65 and 71 all have clusters.

Big Texan Inn   MOTEL $

(☑800-657-7177; www.bigtexan.com; 7700 I-40 E, exit 74; r $50-90; ✴🛏📶♿🐾) The hotel part of Amarillo's star attraction has 54 surprisingly modest rooms behind a faux Old West facade. The real highlight – besides the modest prices – is the outside pool in the shape of Texas. Should you try the huge steak challenge, even crawling across the parking lot to collapse in your room may be beyond you.

Microtel Inn & Suites   MOTEL $

(☑806-372-8373; www.microtelinn.com; 1501 Ross St, off I-40 at exit 71; r $70-100; ✴@📶🛏♿🐾) A typical outlet for this high-scoring budget chain. Rooms are spread over two stories off interior hallways. 'Suites' are really just larger rooms, but for a small rate increase (often just $10) you get a room that sleeps four easily plus has a fridge and microwave.

Hampton Inn   MOTEL $$
(☑806-372-1425; www.hamptoninn.com; 1700 I-40 E, east of exit 71 on south side; r $80-140; ❋ ☎ ☒ ☎) A standard outlet of the always comfortable and reliable midrange chain. Guests enjoy a full breakfast.

Parkview House   B&B $$
(☑806-373-9464; www.parkviewhousebb.com; 1311 S Jefferson St; r $85-135; ❋ ☎) This old Victorian B&B is in a neighborhood of historic homes dating to the cattle-baron days. In addition to five guest rooms and a cottage, it has music- and world-travel themed common rooms. There's a hot tub and a hammock in the yard, and genial Elwood Park is a short stroll away.

Ambassador Hotel   HOTEL $$
(☑800-817-0521, 806-358-6161; www.ambassador amarillo.com; 3100 I-40 W near exit 68; r $100-160; ❋ @ ☎ ☒ ☎) Ignore its stark exterior (unless you're fascinated by the grain silos) and concentrate on the multitude of services offered at this independent hotel aimed at business travelers. The 263 rooms over 10 stories have numerous plush touches and those in the 'Cattle Baron' class are even better.

✖ Eating & Drinking

At first burp, Amarillo seems awash in chain eateries along the I-40 frontage roads, but delve a little deeper to find some gems, especially along SW 6th Ave. However, don't close your eyes to everything on I-40, as Amarillo's top attraction, the Big Texan, awaits.

★ **Golden Light Cafe & Cantina**   BURGERS $
(☑806-374-0097; 2908 SW 6th Ave; mains $4-8; ☺ cafe 11am-10pm, bar 4pm-2am) Classic cheeseburgers, home-cut fries and cold beer have sated travelers on Route 66 at this modest brick dive since 1946. On most nights there's live country and rock music in the atmospherically sweaty cantina next door.

Cowboy Gelato   AMERICAN $
(☑806-376-5286; 2806 SW 6th Ave; treats from $2; ☺11am-8pm Mon-Sat) The Texas plains are flat as a frying pan and often just as hot. Escape the heat in this cute little cafe which makes

Big Texan Steak Ranch
DENNIS MACDONALD / GETTY IMAGES ©

its own creamy gelati. Barbecue sandwiches and fried green beans fill out a meal.

806   CAFE $
(☑806-322-1806; www.the806.com; 2812 SW 6th Ave; mains from $5; ☺8am-midnight; ☎ ☒) Wobbly, mismatched chairs define the funky vibe at this coffeehouse, where local hipsters ponder moving to New York. Beer in bottles plus lots of tasty, healthy snacks such as chili and hummus provide fuel for thought. It has live acoustic music some nights.

Stockyard Cafe   AMERICAN $
(☑806-374-6024; 100 S Manhattan St; mains $5-15; ☺9am-2pm Mon-Thu, to 8pm Fri) This cafe in the Amarillo Livestock Auction building is where the cattlefolk sit down for some beef. The steaks are ideal – thick and perfectly charred – but most have the plate-swamping chicken-fried steak. Follow your nose here, past corrals and railroad tracks.

★ **Big Texan Steak Ranch**   STEAKHOUSE $$
(www.bigtexan.com; 7701 I-40 E, exit 74; mains $10-40; ☺7am-10:30pm; ♠) A classic, hokey Route 66 roadside attraction, the Big Texan made the move when I-40 opened in 1971 and has never looked back. Stretch-Cadillac limos with steer-horn hood ornaments offer free shuttles to and from area motels, marquee lights blink above, a shooting arcade pings inside the saloon, and a big, tall Tex road sign welcomes you (after taunting billboards for miles in either direction).

Amarillo

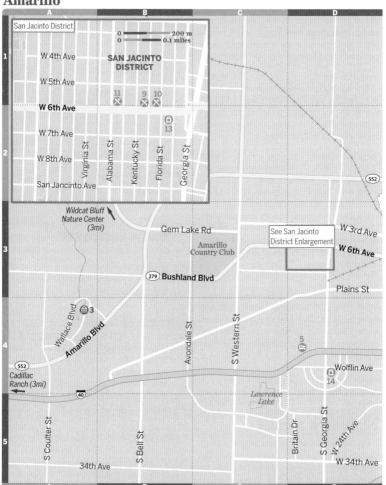

Amarillo

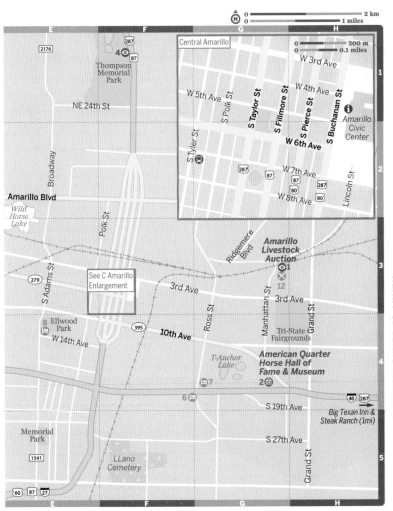

🛍 Shopping

The stretch of SW 6th Ave west of Georgia St has numerous antique and junk shops that recall the old Route 66 beat.

6th Street Antique Mall ANTIQUES
(📞806-374-0459; 2715 SW 6th Ave; ⊙10am-6pm Mon-Sat) Anchors a strip of antique stores.

Boots 'n Jeans WESTERN WEAR
(📞806-353-4368; 2225 S. Georgia St; ⊙9am-6pm Mon-Sat, 11am-6pm Sun) A one-store-only local legend (although it is now owned by retail giant Sheplers), Boots 'n Jeans leaves little

about its inventory to the imagination. Some Panhandle locals will only shop here.

❶ Information

The *Amarillo Independent* is a frisky free weekly with full local event info and an alternative viewpoint.

Amarillo Convention and Visitor Council
(📞806-374-1497, 800-692-1338; www.visit amarillotx.com; Amarillo Civic Center, 401 S Buchanan St; ⊙9am-5pm Mon-Fri year-round, noon-4pm Sat Sep-May, 10am-4pm Sat & Sun Jun-Aug) The staff will be mighty glad you stopped.

123

Driving in Southwest USA

The interstate system is thriving in the Southwest, but a well-maintained network of state roads and scenic byways offers unparalleled opportunities for exploration.

Driving Fast Facts

➡ **Right or Left?** Drive on the right.

➡ **Legal Driving Age** 16 (New Mexico: 15½)

➡ **Top Speed Limit** 85 mph (Hwy 130 between Austin and San Antonio, TX)

➡ **Best Bumper Sticker** We're all here because we're not all there (Jerome, AZ)

DRIVER'S LICENSE & DOCUMENTS

All drivers must carry a driver's license, the car registration and proof of insurance. If your license is not in English, an official translation or an international driving permit (IDP) is highly recommended. You will also need a credit card in order to rent a car.

INSURANCE

Liability insurance covers people and property that you might harm in an accident. For damage to your own rental vehicle, a collision damage waiver (CDW) is available for about $22 to $27 per day. If you have liability and collision coverage on your vehicle at home, it might cover damages to rental cars; inquire before departing. Additionally, some credit cards offer reimbursement coverage for collision damages when you use the card to rent a car; again, ask before departing. There may be exceptions for rentals of more than 15 days or for exotic models, SUVs, vans and 4WD vehicles.

Note that many rental agencies stipulate that damage a car suffers while being driven on unpaved roads is not covered by the insurance it offers. Check with the agent when you make your reservation.

RENTING A CAR

Rental cars are readily available at airports and many downtown city locations. Rates usually include unlimited mileage, but 'unlimited' can actually be capped. Dropping off the car at a different location is usually more expensive than returning it to the place of rental. Larger companies don't require a credit card deposit, which means you can cancel without a penalty if you find a better rate. Since deals abound and the business is competitive, it pays to shop around.

Most companies require that you have a major credit card, are at least 25 years old and have a valid driver's license. Some national agencies may rent to drivers between the ages of 21 and 25 but may charge an additional daily fee.

The following companies operate in the Southwest:

Alamo (www.alamo.com)

Avis (www.avis.com)

Budget (www.budget.com)

Dollar (www.dollar.com)

Hertz (www.hertz.com)

National (www.national.com)

Thrifty (www.thrifty.com)

BORDER CROSSING

Cities and towns in Arizona where you can cross the Mexican–US border include San Luis (south of Yuma), Lukeville (Hwy 85), Nogales and Douglas. From New Mexico, travel south to El Paso, TX, to reach Ciudad Juárez. US Customs and Border Protection tracks current wait times (see http://apps.cbp.gov/bwt) at every border crossing.

Bring your passport if you are crossing the border. Foreign visitors should review US entry requirements at the State Department (www.travel.state.gov) and the US Customs and Border Protection (www.cbp.gov) websites.

MAPS

Detailed state highway maps are distributed free by state governments. Call or send an email to state tourism offices

Road-Trip Websites

American Automobile Association (AAA; ☏800-222-4357; www.aaa.com) Provides maps and other information, as well as travel discounts and 24-hour emergency assistance for members.

America's Byways (www.byways.org) Descriptions and maps for designated national scenic byways.

Gas Buddy (www.gasbuddy.com) Find the cheapest gas in town.

Roadside America (www.roadside america.com) Strange and wonderful things in Texas towns large and small.

Historic Route 66 (www.historic 66.com) The historic way across the Panhandle.

Southwest USA Playlist

Border Town Chris Whitley

Rocky Mountain High John Denver

Take it Easy The Eagles

Texas, Texas Red Meat

Viva Las Vegas Elvis Presley

(typically through their websites) to request maps, or pick them up at highway tourism information offices when you enter a state on a major highway. For exploring Native American reservations in the Four Corners region, buy the popular AAA Indian Country map. It's for sale at **Books 'n' More** (☺8am-8pm Jun-Aug, vary rest of the year), which is across the plaza from Grand Canyon Visitor Center on the South Rim, and from various outlets online.

ROADS & CONDITIONS

Be extra defensive while driving in the Southwest. Everything from dust storms to snow to roaming livestock can make conditions dangerous. Near Flagstaff, watch for elk at sunset on I-17 – they like to soak up warmth from the blacktop (or so we heard). Elk can weigh between 500lb and 900lb.

Distances are great in the Southwest and there are long stretches of road without gas stations. Running out of gas on a hot and desolate stretch of highway is no fun, so pay attention to signs that caution 'Next Gas 98 Miles.'

Road conditions for interstates and rural highways are typically very good. Unpaved roads to ghost towns, petroglyph sites, and remote trailheads are generally well-graded but can be challenging after storms or if they lead to very remote sites. Unpaved roads across Indian reservations are of varying quality. Consider using 4WD vehicles for extended trips on dirt roads and ask locally about conditions.

For updates on road conditions, call ☏511 (excluding Texas) while traveling within the state, or call one of the following:
Arizona (☏in-state 511, 888-411-7623; www.az511.com)
Nevada (☏in-state 511, 877-687-6237; www.nvroads.com)

New Mexico (📱in-state 511, 800-432-4269; http://nmroads.com)
Southern Colorado (📱in-state 511, 303-639-1111; www.cotrip.org)
Texas (📱800-452-9292)
Utah (📱in-state 511, 866-511-8824; www.commuterlink.utah.gov)

your location, watch for speed limit signs requiring a lower speed than the maximums listed here.

Texting while driving is banned for all drivers in Colorado, Nevada and Utah. Hand-held cell phone use is banned in Nevada.

ROAD RULES

Driving laws are slightly different in each state, but all require the use of safety belts. In every state, children under five years of age must ride in a child safety seat secured by proper restraints.

The maximum speed limit on all rural interstates is 75mph, with Texas and Utah allowing higher speeds on a handful of specified sections of road. The speed limit drops to 65mph in urban areas in Arizona, Colorado, Nevada and Utah. New Mexico and Texas allow urban interstate drivers to barrel through at 75mph. But no matter

PARKING

Public parking is readily available in most Southwest destinations, whether on the street or in parking lots. In rural areas and small towns it is often free of charge. Many towns have metered parking, which will limit the amount of time you can leave your car.

Parking can be a challenge in urban areas. Street parking is limited so you will probably have to pay to leave your car in private lots. See the City Guides, p10, for more information about parking in San Antonio and Austin.

Road Distances (miles)

	Amarillo, TX	Austin, TX	Bryce Canyon NP, UT	Carlsbad, NM	Cortez (Mesa Verde NP), CO	Denver, CO	Grand Canyon (North Rim), AZ	Grand Canyon (South Rim), AZ	Las Vegas, NV	Phoenix, AZ	Reno, NV	Salt Lake City, UT	Santa Fe, NM
Austin, TX	495												
Bryce Canyon NP, UT	835	1250											
Carlsbad, NM	285	480	820										
Cortez (Mesa Verde NP), CO	540	960	390	530									
Denver, CO	435	930	565	580	380								
Grand Canyon (North Rim), AZ	750	1175	130	740	340	690							
Grand Canyon (South Rim), AZ	695	1110	290	685	370	675	210						
Las Vegas, NV	855	1300	250	850	570	755	270	280					
Phoenix, AZ	705	1005	430	590	400	790	340	220	290				
Reno, NV	1305	1740	565	1295	840	990	680	725	450	735			
Salt Lake City, UT	880	1300	260	870	350	520	390	520	420	710	520		
Santa Fe, NM	280	700	660	270	280	390	530	470	640	520	1080	630	
Tucson, AZ	735	890	540	480	470	890	470	350	410	120	855	820	560

Driving Problem-Buster

What should I do if my car breaks down? Call the service number provided by the rental-car company, and it will make arrangements with a local garage. If you're driving your own car, its advisable to join AAA (p125), which provides emergency assistance.

What if I have an accident? If serious damage occurs, you'll have to call the local police (☎911) to come to the scene of the accident and file an accident report, for insurance purposes.

What should I do if I get stopped by the police? Always pull over to the right at the first available opportunity. Stay in your car and roll down the window. Show the officer your driver's license and automobile registration. For any violations, you cannot pay the officer for the ticket; payment must be made by mail or online.

What happens at a border patrol checkpoint? The 'stop side' of the checkpoint is the route going from the south (Mexico) to the north (USA). You may be waved through; otherwise, slow down, stop and answer a few questions (regarding your citizenship and the nature of your visit) and possibly pop your trunk and roll down your window so that the officers can see into your car.

What if I can't find anywhere to stay? In summer it's advisable to make reservations in advance. Most towns have tourist information centers or chambers of commerce that will help travelers find accommodation in a pinch. Public lands managed by the Bureau of Land Management and the forest service often allow dispersed camping, which means you can camp where you want on undeveloped land as long as you stay 900ft from a developed water source and follow other guidelines (www.blm.gov).

FUEL

Gas stations are common in urban areas and along interstates. Many are open 24 hours a day. Small-town stations may be open only from 7am to 8pm or 9pm.

At most stations, you must pay before you pump. The more modern pumps have credit-/debit-card terminals built into them, so you can pay right at the pump. At more expensive, 'full service' stations, an attendant will pump your gas for you; no tip is expected.

SAFETY

When leaving the car, travelers are advised to remove valuables and lock all car doors, especially in urban areas and at isolated trailheads. Be extra careful driving on rural roads at night, which may not be well-lit and may be populated by deer, elk, livestock and other creatures, which can often total your car if you hit them.

RADIO

Arizona On the Hopi reservation KUYI (88.1FM) plays reggae, honky tonk, Cajun and Native American music, with Hopi news.

New Mexico KTAO (101.9FM) in Taos is a solar-powered station airing Native American music, astrology reports, local news, outlaw country and world music.

Texas In Lubbock, KDAV (1590AM), where Buddy Holly once worked, plays nothing but classic rockabilly.

BEHIND THE SCENES

SEND US YOUR FEEDBACK

We love to hear from travellers – your comments help make our books better. We read every word, and we guarantee that your feedback goes straight to the authors. Visit **lonelyplanet.com/contact** to submit your updates and suggestions.

Note: We may edit, reproduce and incorporate your comments in Lonely Planet products such as guidebooks, websites and digital products, so let us know if you don't want your comments reproduced or your name acknowledged. For a copy of our privacy policy visit lonelyplanet.com/privacy.

ACKNOWLEDGMENTS

Climate map data adapted from Peel MC, Finlayson BL & McMahon TA (2007) 'Updated World Map of the Köppen-Geiger Climate Classification', *Hydrology and Earth System Sciences*, 11, pp1633–44.

Cover photographs: Front: Bluebonnets in bloom, Danita Delimont/Getty; Back: Musician David Harris performs in Luckenbach, Danita Delimont/AWL

THIS BOOK

This 1st edition of *San Antonio, Austin & Texas Backcountry Road Trips* was researched and written by Amy C Balfour, Lisa Dunford, Mariella Krause, Regis St Louis and Ryan Ver Berkmoes. This guidebook was produced by the following:

Product Editor Kate Chapman

Senior Cartographer Alison Lyall

Cartographers Mick Garrett, Julie Sheridan, Diana von Holdt

Book Designer Cam Ashley

Cover Researcher Naomi Parker

Thanks to Shahara Ahmed, Sasha Baskett, Brendan Dempsey, Bruce Evans, Ryan Evans, James Hardy, Anne Mason, Catherine Naghten, Darren O'Connell, Katie O'Connell, Kirsten Rawlings, Kathryn Rowan, Victoria Smith, Angela Tinson, Tony Wheeler

OUR STORY

A beat-up old car, a few dollars in the pocket and a sense of adventure. In 1972 that's all Tony and Maureen Wheeler needed for the trip of a lifetime – across Europe and Asia overland to Australia. It took several months, and at the end – broke but inspired – they sat at their kitchen table writing and stapling together their first travel guide, *Across Asia on the Cheap*. Within a week they'd sold 1500 copies. Lonely Planet was born.

Today, Lonely Planet has offices in Melbourne, London and Oakland, with more than 600 staff and writers. We share Tony's belief that 'a great guidebook should do three things: inform, educate and amuse'.

INDEX

000 Map pages

OUR WRITERS

MARIELLA KRAUSE

Mariella first fell in love with Austin when she checked out the UT campus during her junior year of high school. After college, she intended to live 'everywhere,' but felt so at home in Austin that she accidentally stayed for 15 years. Mariella will always consider Texas home, and she still sprinkles her language with Texanisms whenever possible, much to the amusement of those who don't consider 'y'all' a legitimate pronoun.

REGIS ST LOUIS

A Hoosier by birth, Regis grew up in a sleepy riverside town where he dreamed of big-city intrigue. He's lived all over the US (including New York City, San Francisco, Los Angeles and New Orleans), and has crossed the country by train, bus and car while visiting remote corners of America. Favorite memories from his most recent trip include crab feasting on Maryland's eastern shore, hiking through striking state parks in west Texas, catching music jams in the Blue Ridge Mountains of Virginia and going eye-to-eye with wild horses on Assateague Island. Regis has contributed to more than 50 Lonely Planet titles, including New York City and Washington, DC.

AMY C BALFOUR

Amy has hiked, biked, skied and gambled her way across the Southwest. She has authored or co-authored more than 15 books for Lonely Planet and has written for *Backpacker*, *Every Day with Rachael Ray*, *Redbook*, *Southern Living* and *Women's Health*.

LISA DUNFORD

Does living in a state for 22 years, marrying a native and learning to speak the language mean someone can become a naturalized Texan? Lisa sure hopes so. Over the years she's logged tens of thousands of miles exploring her adopted home. She loves cruising the country roads seeing what there is to see – a cow in a bluebonnet field, or an old barnlike dance hall. She's bought boys drinks at the Continental Club in Austin, ridden the rides at the State Fair in Dallas and sailed on Corpus Christi Bay. Before becoming a freelance writer, Lisa was a restaurant reviewer and an editor in the features department at the Corpus Christi Caller-Times newspaper. Now no matter where she roams, she always returns to the patch of riverfront east of Houston that she, her husband and their dogs call home.

RYAN VER BERKMOES

Ryan grew up in Santa Cruz, California, the sort of goofball beachtown place that made him immediately love Port Aransas. An inveterate wanderer, he was most at home on the hundreds of miles of Texas backroads he traversed for research. Whether it was discovering a forgotten town on Texas Hwy 70 or driving to the literal end of the road to (happily!) check out still another empty Gulf Coast beach, he relished every click on the odometer.

Published by Lonely Planet Publications Pty Ltd
ABN 36 005 607 983
1st edition – May 2016
ISBN 978 1 76034 049 0
© Lonely Planet 2016   Photographs © as indicated 2016
10 9 8 7 6 5 4 3 2 1
Printed in China